£18

Copyright © 2021 Kenning JP García

Published in the year 2021 in the country of the United States of America in the state of Washington and the cavity of Seattle by the publisher Really Serious Literature.

All rights reserved. No part of this publication may be reproduced without the express written consent of the author.

Cover Art by François Luong

ISBN: 978-0-578-33750-0

"Kenning JP García is one of the most innovative, most important writers we have right now. They are a personal hero to me, an icon, someone whose work I always keep an eye on. Kenning doesn't push boundaries because that implies their work is still limited by boundaries. Kenning knows all about boundaries, but does not waste time on them. With is that kind of work, something people will label and mislabel over and over again. It isn't even a book to me. It's something more important. It's an interjection. A shard lodging itself into the outline of my life until my body is reformed, letting me know new beautiful things are being born, even if I don't yet know its name."

Chiwan Choi, author of *THE YELLOW HOUSE*

"Sad, lovely and as always whip smart, García's WITH contains sharp, complex lines, "Some cafés are all chatter. Kindness comes in odd dosages. Strangers ain't so bad when one gets sad enough to settle for anybody." This diary/anti-poetry collection will stick with you for the long haul"

Erika T. Wurth, author of *WHITEHORSE*

"The world ghosts the ghosts it gives life to." So states the speaker of Kenning JP García's restlessly experimental With, which hovers in the space between poetry and prose — between "diary" and "antipoetry," as the title asserts. Throughout, García exhibits a remarkable capacity for innovation, deploying puns, slant rhymes, and other forms of sonic play to induce a vertiginous semiosis that leaves the reader "ghosted" between shadows of potential meaning. In the spectral interchange between signifier and sign, then, is a desire to think one meaning with another, one semantic layer pressed sometimes uncomfortably against the next. In so doing, García offers an incisive exploration not only of the fraught nature of meaning-making, but of our (we come to find) unsettled notions of what it means to think and be."

John James, author of *THE MILK HOURS*

"This book reaches over and dips its fries in your frosty, and you're ok with that, because the book says *fuck you,* but ina cool way, and all you can say is… You got it. Kenning JP García has got it in a way none of the rest of us do."

Kelsey Marie Harris, author of *BURY YOUR HORSES*, *SPIT (VERB) IN MY MOUTH*, and *SEX WOUND*

"'All stories are ghost stories and all letters are love letters or maybe it's some other way around,' writes Kenning JP Garcia. And this book is, at once, ghost story and love letter. Each entry seems epistolary in quality, but the drift of mind is ephemeral. I am delighted to examine each new twist beyond the next asterisk. A haunting literary exposition."

Kyle McCord, author of *REUNION OF THE GOOD WEATHER SUICIDE CULT*

Some of this work has been published in Snail Trail Press and by the Magnificent Field.

Thanks.

WITH

(diary / antipoetry)

by

Kenning JP García

2020

But the stars tell lies, it blinds the only warning

And when darkness dies, there's nothing left but morning . . .

Just day and night

Day and night . . . the shadows start to scatter

When touched by light . . . each promise made is shattered

And even when the question find the answer

But even then...

Jim Carroll - Day and Night

Dusk

"... to be cleansed of question. / But not of seeking..." (Ed Roberson)

Comfort is an empty church. Skin on skin never felt the way it was supposed to. The way it was described from the classics to the contemporaries. Some sorts of things are not good at creating good impressions, first or otherwise.

*

Tonight will always feel longer than any yesterday.

*

"The world is impossible ... Let it go." (Laziness - Andrei Voznesensky)

*

"Blessed is laziness ... too lazy to get up, or fall back asleep ... Progress is laziness." (Laziness - Andrei Voznesensky)

Intuition tells on itself. Sells itself out for lowest bidders. Just wants to speak up. Be heard. But beware, once a vision is seen, it's compromised.

Thought about how plots took a moment to plan. Fucked up an outline for a night. Flirted among sketches. But it's always only a fling. Nothing lasts. Not even the shit that started it all. The world is warmer than was heard or maybe travel is just another short term solution to the seasons.

What that nigga say in that one Goines' joint? "A new day is necessary." Yeah, one that starts in the black. Can't take no more of this red. Been fucked up. Been fed up. But can remember before being drunk. Before being pissed about how much longer the night was made by hunger. Couldn't wait to be uppity but downfall always got in the way. It's a world held tight by a core never giving up surfaces.

Waves rise up then curl, fold over, fall. But break? Daybreak snaps the night and breakfast ends the fasting that sleep has created but break? Where are the words that feel closer to what the world feels as actions take place? As actions take places? Become outlines more so than details?

*

This shouldn't be real. It's hopeful that it's not. Nothing is good. Even less is fair. Reality does its best at middling. The centricity of zeroes zero in on here. This is here. That is there. There is this. Here is that. Absolute values will be shown absolutely by distance achieved. By proximity approved.

It's always before the after. It's always after the before. A morning after. There has to be one at the end of the day.

*

Brightest.

*

Take a minute. Indulge. Divest. Look around. Exit the smells that don't excuse that sounds. That don't complement the touch of an aroma that stays in touch. Calls and recalls. Was that meat on a grill? It might not have been. Faint is a problem full of pressures pressing down in faded attempts at recognition. Or the sense itself betrays itself.

*

There's a letter to right. To the letter. Letter of the law. An uncorrected proof is circulating. Old yet serviceable. Still works. Gets something done. Puts the "ish" in finish. Is close enough. Is good enough when fair enough has gone on holiday.

*

But when it comes time to keep it real, where is real for the keeping? Out the window. Ain't out on the street at this time unless it's looking for a lesson. Fear comes fast. Anxiety is a catcall. Dread a catchall. The wind wolf whistles worries into actualities.

*

Can't find the hips to fit the jeans of this mood.

*

Hunger stresses over the sensation of being waylaid. There's a hunt. It's on. Stay dissatisfied. What one lacks an other retains. Keeps on retainer. Desire works pro bono. There's always a case where the spirit becomes its own ambulance.

*

Never been introduced. Wouldn't change anything any way. It's cold in the alleys. Cold in slim places tonight. Freezing where souls go to vacate. Neither made nor destroyed means on the job. At task. Energy running low on energy. What could remain so energized for so long as forever?

The world ghosts the ghosts it gives life to. Strings itself along for a while. Plays, no, uses its own emotions until the rush runs out.

*

There's a wall that won't hold up itself. A wall in want of a flower. A flower still on the prey for birds and bees to lend a helping hand or whatever limb can be lent out. Be of use.

*

Is this the look of fun? Fuck! Where's the hood at? Switch up the dynamics. Shift the paradigm back to the ghetto where the sentimentality was first destroyed but the mentality was born.

It's all immaterial. Been found by nefarious means. Memory is notorious for going around the rules to get the evidence it doesn't deserve.

*

Oh, loosen up.

*

Tears are in eyes and what if Jesus never laughed and Socrates never cried? What if false wasn't untrue? Whose defenses are down? Every day has been lead astray down the detours of songs and memes and too many videos left to view. Curiosity lives in the queue. Up next is another clue but an angel has never been sent. This is real life but it's not the decade one grew up in anymore. It's the future that was foretold of inaccurately. The devil is in the details of the mistakes. Errors are demons that will never be dispossessed and it's 2 slices and a soda for $5 at the place on the corner or more further down the block. It's a pint of lo mein for a little more and a bagel for a little less. It's tacos about the same and it's starving for free and another drink on somebody familiar at the bar. It's not where anybody grew up but where people reside. Schoolyard dreams fell in the cracks between childhood and the highway miles lost getting to another beer. E&J afternoons on the subway gave way to PBR in dives. Plotting doesn't always live up to planning.

*

Can't stop the world. The future was wide but it's closing now. About halfway through life if all goes well enough to keep going and there's not much to think about in the glimmer coming through slimmest of cracks. Aliens enter in unpredictable ways. Maybe another dimension is at the other end of these thoughts. Maybe not. Maybe this is the other dimension. One of many others. Where's the hood at? Where's the old courtyard? Where's the stoop and the stories? Where's six flights up and a broken elevator? Where's the smell? And a bannister uncomfortable in little hands? Still tired today from all that walking.

*

How hard was it to turn away? Turn pirate? Turn western? Take to the sea? Take to the trail? Is this that kind of story? Is adventure what's needed or more mystery? Is there a mission or just a journey? The sails are filling and the horses are getting antsy. Or maybe squirrely. No animal adjectives or adverbs, yes adverbs, feel adequate. No adverbs. Time to turn heel on all those descriptors of actions. Turn villain. There are no heroes here not even a protagonist. Go sing in the dark if sirens are better suited to this story.

*

Happy birthday to newborn fears.

*

There have to be more words than these currently available. So much self-awareness comes accompanied by jibber-jabber. As for actualization, what comes alongside that? Nothing painted blue. Even less borrowed. Even less old. Always room for something new. When's the wedding?

*

Sorry has some regrets. The backlash has some resentments to take care of. To raise and turn into responsible adults capable of being able to become productive members of society and maybe even be good parents to little resentments to come. The winds have changed. Decided the look wasn't working and who pays up but those lost at sea? A good pirate never gets lost though. Follow the sun and stars. Ask the gut for some more applause when shore becomes another temporary home. A narrative will always find a way.

*

Sorry for existing in this world while ghosts don't but by virtue of that create a cruel symmetry that this cosmos so requested. Or ghosts exist and this idea does not. There is no voice to prove that this thought has been said. It was never said. May never be said. And it's lonely living in a universe devoid of spirits to guide but at least hell is personal. And has personality too. Aliens have eyes everywhere. Androids are reprogrammed as bugs are discovered. Life is a trial run. A test drive, innocent in its ignorance of its own issues.

*

The dead have a day. Mourners reach out for otherworldly affection. Senses sit around waiting to take the witness stand. Ready to be questioned.

Feed a fever. Starve an apparition.

Melodrama is a perfect and natural fit to play the role as head of a haunted household. There's no argument to be had amongst the members.

*

All stories are ghost stories and all letters are love letters or maybe it's some other way around. A different combination of the notions.

*

Is it time to give it a rest? Is there room for a nap? Is this the way to approach restlessness? Who will agree to this bargain? Each choice occurs freely, greedily, trying desperately to bring the adverbs back. Jokes try to make light of the listlessness. Who is listening? Who is eavesdropping on indecision? Who is ear hustling in on the interiority of dreams? Lucidity has let itself go and is now a mass of confused languages while disgust spends its time drying out the lips. Codes whisper and say, "takes one to know one" while switching places.

*

Wake up, smell the flowers when flowers can be found. Won't no flowers back in the day. Still ain't many now. Who put all this concrete everywhere? Makes it hard to concentrate but there's lots to think about. Dwell on.

*

"When life seems hopeless / It make a nigga lose focus / Empty beer bottles and roaches"

(Ludacris - Hopeless)

*

"...still that piece of drifting wood..." (Ernest Gaines) still and so on looking for better rivers, streams, creeks, and brooks. Looking for beds and shores. Something ready to erode but not just yet. Want to share both transience and temporality. Nobody knows all there is to know about duration but it's a talk to be had.

Death can be forgiven. Endings are apologies also. Sorrow runs both ways. When it's over, it is what it was destined to be. Fate comes to fruition one way or another. And the ultimate conclusion gets no love except in those cases, those times when the eviction from this existence couldn't come fast enough. Who deserved to go sooner? Ask these scars, nigga.

Hand to God. Hands up. Square up. It's time to go. Long overdue. What was all that breaking bread at the same table as the enemy when the body was being handed out Sunday after Sunday?

*

What fortune is there to be found in the end? Found out in the end? All is lost. Woe is death. Woe is survival too. Woe is every meal.

*

Just kidding. Maybe.

*

Raised on the look out. Grew into a decoy. Ain't seen shit. Don't say shit. Or say so much it has the sound of coming out the neck. All bullshit. All signifying. Learned the rules of that syntax, those semantics. The tongue is a terrible thing to taste. Too much kept on it. Not enough spat back out. Fingers got to take up a certain amount of slack.

*

Two dead parents and a dead end job. Two options – angry or sad. The dialectic doesn't offer up enjoyment anymore. Or, maybe that's bullshit too. A new con the ghetto forgot to teach its youth. Or, perhaps sympathy ain't nothing but some sort of white folks Wile E Coyote type of scheming. Don't worry, it'll all come together someday but not someday soon. It's been a jigsaw life. It'll be a crosswords future.

*

Plant-based guilt puts down roots. Never planned to end up here, this way, such as this here thinking about all the ways to lessen suffering in a world that doesn't care about anybody's suffering. The world isn't cruel, just apathetic. The world itself. The land, sea, and air can't accommodate everybody. The world as far as people go, well there's always more betrayal to come. That's not indifferent. That's very specific so maybe there were some lies in what has been said here even if it wasn't heard. Honesty isn't as readily available as it should be. Its absence is a cause of suffering. It's a seed, this lacking, that expands, grows and eventually bears fruit of more emptiness. A loss too untempting to taste but alongside a feeling that is unavoidable.

*

Maybe one day all consciousness will just fade away. Die and be sought after by grief or faith or whomever enjoys the afterlife less. Whoever goes to the other side has to come back having a new consciousness reborn by what was seen among the shadows.

Headline: Beyond vegan burgers: next-generation protein could come from air, methane, volcanic springs.

So, is reading or thinking more helpful right now?

*

Where's the initiative? Been back and forth on getting going. Want it all. Want all the go and all the stay. Need a moment for a new mood to get uncomfortable. Let a mood get too big for the room so that there's no choice but to leave. That's one way to get going. That's what the wrong side of the bed is for.

*

Just the other day Curiosity took pictures of its "prison" on Mars.

"The broken blade is the Negro." (Virginia Woolf - the Waves) How broken? A clean break or a jagged edge left as a reminder of the snap and separation.

This is the beginning again, vague and pointless yet the story remains poignant or becomes so. Before is near to after. The distance between the two is negligible. And it's becoming harder to remember. Recollection has a feel, a texture, and a heft. Firm but malleable. Volume switches. Width is aleatory and up for grabs to the highest bidder. What does not bid on before to get at after? After is so desperate. After owns a precise loneliness and action or inactivity. Next shifts and interrupts the perfection that has already left and has been away for far too long now.

The phrase stays the same in the presence of all-consuming quotation marks but finds refuge in cage of parentheses and the clause assembled in the face of sensation. Sensing loses its center in the name of love. The places see the line growing and slowing. Before must be torn asunder while after is minus, a cornerstone. No foundation. Slippery slope upon which to build a new church.

*

This is the ending again. Watch out for circumstances swimming upstream to spawn.

*

Clear the history. Leave no trace of searches. Give no impression. Blow no hot air into deflated ideas. Don't hammer out dents nor details. Learn to appreciate the flatness of things. Think items into easier to examine dimensions.

The clanging of the bell brings no clarity to the twee daydreams. Telenovelas become commercials for Tide and Ivory Snow. The game is under the spell of the referee's whistle. Dancehall and battle rap move to the meters measured out by airhorns. What sounds shook griots from the chronicling?

*

Ain't nobody out here trying to pay a nigga – half or otherwise – to think these things in Spanglish, patois, or any kind of vernacular creased so much so to turn the whiteness of an imaginary page to black. Upon the creases, blackness being the history of folding. The pocket asked for pages. Now the pocket answers more to screens. Blackness dragged out flat across the surface of the machine – off. Time to reconsider what has or has yet to be seen. Come on, nigga, cheer up. Think of all the contacts in that phone. Gotta be somebody good in there.

*

This job ain't shit.

*

This recycled air is on elbows exposed while hands are in gloves but ready for the time clock to announce the divorce.

*

"If this is all, this is worthless ... Where then is the break in this continuity?" (Virginia Woolf - the Waves)

There are memes to an end. There's a rhythm to this repetition. A tempo to the killing of time, one picture at a time, familiar and new. An ephemeral cliché – changing slightly for the sake of some laughs. Are these worth it while ignoring the tasks still up late at this hour of all hours at the end of the day, darkest before the after? The seasons resurrect some classics. The winter is a genre in and **of** itself. Back to work. Why can't the sticker just remain where it lay? What a waste of art. It was art wasn't it? The stuff of labels are art, right? Upstairs, downstairs. Instairs, outstairs. Where is

Buckminster for an answer? Fuller is dead again before these questions.

Inquiries ripple at the edge of the inscapes where outside and inside meet where boats set sail and dock. Where nobody forgets about the pirates mentioned earlier in the night.

*

Better off dead than asleep. No good to anybody in bed or anywhere caught up in the solace of a nap. Death at least is something to rally the troops. Martyrs are motivation and can be made from captains and scallywags alike.

*

Replenished!?! Not even sleep can replenish dreams. Rest is not worth the work it takes to get to sleep but to stay in bed all day is a fantasy fulfilled.

Or quite the opposite. The protagonist has been removed from the story. One pity does not lead to another. Pity is not a bronco to bust. What value does a buckaroo have on this prairie? On this ranch or on this cattle drive? It's a rodeo of emotions. This is no place for a greenhorn.

*

A picture is not a fact. There are portfolios full of lies. Movies are yarns spun out. Moving falsities that have helped form this and here as reality reflects the art of the sequential and visual con arts. The only truth is the staging. The rest is a beautiful betrayal. Facts are hard to trust when there are so many feelings to contest. Conjecture and debate arise to ask what works? Whatever works is held onto forever. Ghosts, gods, aliens. Sorrow, anger, and joy until one enters the after or returns to the before. One is a time traveler as time traveling is needed. One needs a relief from when as well as where.

One is an accountant and actuary of the selves and the otherness of those selves.

*

This life is only commandeered. The ghetto is full of privateers but not thugs. That chaos isn't there as the original definition spoke to. The chaos is the wind and waves while the rest is orderly under a special set of rules. The weather may be rough or calm, the money flowing, vessels pass by, pass through, everybody gotta keep it moving. Can't stall for the unexpected. Adapt and get while the getting is good. Get an attitude to fit the environment. The local conditions aren't competition. It's all setting. The actor acts. The speech acts also.

*

Death rattles. Death grips. Makes a spectacle of itself and its undying loyalty. Unconditional love. The end and the conclusion are indifferent to one another and the coda is all artificial ingredients. Selves die everyday. Others exist. Continue to exist. Then don't. Before there were others. Afterwards there will be one. The singularity believes in itself and requires no agreement. The horizon has no sense of empathy. One day the event will occur. What happens next will be new or it will be as before.

*

This is all a distraction. Thinking back. Thinking forward. Thinking. Thoughts are sandcastles as the tide looks to rise and the shore readies itself for the hit.

*

Is this all crazy talk? Crazy thoughts? How is one supposed to occur in world made of science and fantasy? The hood and the classics forced upon younger person's understanding of reading?

The blade is broken. The wild horses are not.

Read too many comic books to not consider the multiversity.

The before could be a Western or a swashbuckling tale. The after could be first contact or a result of artificial intelligence. The now might be a shift behind a broom. The broom before the T500e scrubs the tiles. Two floors. Instairs and outstairs needing to be cleaned.

*

The Five Percenters said things that the Black Israelites didn't agree to. Rastas and preachers didn't see eye to eye. The priests read the good book in ways that the Witnesses and the Christian Scientists didn't. The Sephardic folks and practioners of Santería kept secrets never spoken of much out on the streets of youth where the Caribbean was scooped up into a few blocks as buildings were thrown up floor over floor.

The before stumbled on. The after will also.

*

"The heart has its reasons that reason does not know." (Marcel Proust)

*

Actually, a break doesn't stop someone but merely crushes one. The waves break upon the shore. Crushing shells and sand. Bray – To pound or crush fine, as in a mortar. And something new was learned. By assistance of a search as a response to a rebuttal.

What was the shore's answer to the abuse? Donkeys bray. Do mules? Upon further examination, that's a yes and no. A whinny and a bray but not a pure bray. Not a pure bred, not a pure break between the horse and the donkey.

*

"Life ain't a track meet. It's a marathon." (Ice Cube)

*

"Money ain't everything, but somehow eases ... as memories resurface ... Welfare, food stamps, and stealing from the store

Come home ... Can't take no more ... dispersing these feelings ... To know the ending one must understand the prequel..." (Logic)

*

Be home back when the streetlights come on. Be back right after school or at least before anybody **else** gets back in. Straightlaced so far as the stories on the streets go. All laughs. Chuckles and baby weight. Ain't shit gonna be funny when the stacks is feeling light. When the books is cooked. Eat enough crumbs and a nigga can sure as shit feel full. Never feel satisfied but full. Congrats on overlooking the wrong ones. Hope the inventory is looking fucked up now and forever. Lose a little here, miss some shit over there. But ain't nobody over here hungry or bored. Watching the new shit. Reading the latest issues. Pockets got candy for days. Go to school in the morning do it all again a little further away from home next time.

Good / bad don't mean nothing. Not a villain but nemesis sure does sound right in the ears. Might not leave the tongue but eyes would do best to recognize. Consider survival a challenge.

Consider every problem unrelated but a family from a broken home, growing up and getting old together. Stayed in touch. Blood is thicker than water but there ain't no high seas of blood. And three sheets to the wind ain't about the blood but the alcohol.

*

Ever seen a knife in flesh? Ever seen a sibling in a crib at the same time. Ever heard that phone call? Two parents can be a curse in disguise. Blessings counted didn't add up. Were never greater than the sum of the parts. Didn't get here, this before, waiting on an after by keeping the same energy.

"... learned to swallow ... tears and to mistrust sweet words." (Ricardo Güiraldes - Don Segundo Sombra)

"Every saint got a past, every sinner got a future / Every loser gotta win and every winner gotta lose someday" (J Cole)

*

An instrument made for its sound before the sound was ever heard. Here, to line, the lining of a coat never made. Here, predating and predestined. Predetermined. A preposition giving space to verbs and nouns. Ready the dative. Ready the genitive.

*

Orphaned late in life. Nowhere to turn to now.

*

Unintended. Intensions puffed up coats that couldn't keep the cold out. Might as well see how the other side lives. Make some friends. Look for another somewhere to reside. The unintended provides shelters never considered. Thought preparation was the best use of genius. Thought revenge was the stuff of sitcoms and was supposed to be sort of funny. Live in the company of consequences. Love who is nearest if loving is so fucking important.

Don't let locusts forget what was eaten. Don't let English forget what words were given while still further liberties are being taken.

*

This is a love story and a ghost letter. The blade broke trying to separate the two.

Is the fire burning for warmth or for light?

Well, cowpoke, what kind of cows are these? Leather, beef, dairy? So much suffering on the ranch. On the range. Home, home on the range.

*

Night terrors and the pursuit of nothingness. Happiness is a dream that only brings more sleep paralysis. Been on the road more than once, tried to catch some shut eye, met nightmares instead. Couldn't get out. Couldn't get away. Lucidity failed and had to ride it out hoping other passengers weren't subjected to screams from this body. Sensations never sleep. Feelings haunt. Memory is a lover that won't leave when the leaving is good. Recollection is always worse for the wear. Remembrance is worn out. The search is lost but is ready for any emergencies.

Out in the woods stumbling. To trip is human but to fall is angelic.

*

On time and on schedule. In correspondence and accordance under the clock. By comparison, or in proportion to a lack of desire. Don't want to be here. Tired of thriving on misery as Tupac once sang out. And furthermore the hour is ringing in 60 minute increments against all odds who would ask for another 5 minute smoke break.

But rounds are 3 minutes and leave a minute between one another for listening and catching breath. Holding onto a moment of reprieve that the world never willingly wanted to give up but as time is money, entertainment is really big money.

And, there still ain't no war on poverty. Some things will never change.

*

Who is up now? Who wants to talk? Never mind. This is the moment of mourning. No sense in trying to connect.

Checked the email, read about some motherfucker not worth reading about. Not happy for nobody. Set transcendence back by another lifetime. 100 miles and running except the realest nigga was left behind. Never had dinner at the president's house.

Go to bed, these hours ain't for everybody. Work or play. Pleasure is out of the question.

Everywhere except here. Trying to consider better days but where? Can't laugh. Don't play. Even playfights got real way too soon.

*

"Hello. The motherfuckin world is a ghetto." (Ice Cube)

Wanted to switch up attitudes. Gave a lot of other options some opportunities but at the end, in the end, what came before will always exist. The after doesn't get any thanks it will one day get. The before occurred ignored and unappreciated so, here now continues in its own moment owning itself for its own sake. Ain't no reason to give shout outs to other moments. Nostalgia moved out as soon as it could. Found a better neighborhood, got tired of sentimentality always taking the nigga route to keep it real.

Nostalgia and sentimentality came up on the streets together. Was family, cousins, but never was synonyms. Never meant the same thing. Never stood for the same shit.

*

"Nostalgia: a wistful desire to return in thought or in fact to a former time in one's life, to one's home or homeland, or to one's family and friends; a sentimental yearning for the happiness of a former place or time." (Dictionary.com)

Nostalgia needed sentimentality, the sentimental, the sentiment. Sentimentality never asked for any help. Was always about itself. For itself. Except when sentimentality gives in to its own understanding of its own mentality becomes a way of thinking, being, existing. The only way to proceed. To proceed is the after of to occur. It's how the before considers the end of the day. How the darkest is always before.

*

A new day is necessary. No time for like, share, comment. Time to skip the social and the media. Every word gets the scrutiny it deserves as it touches the air aimed at ears, at eyes, avoids touch, taste, smell receives the sixth sense treatment it gets. Vocabulary and semantics willed **to** be **will be** taxed as syntax sees fit.

Not trying to pun through these ideas. Not trying to play words games. Not one for playing. No time for games. Lost too many pieces to the set to keep on playing. Only thing left is the board. The game is broken. This nigga is broke. Every day is work. Every sound is miserable, struggling, suffering to be set free. Free to fight.

*

"Always kept it real from the very start (very start) ... / ... Niggas ain't thorough ... / Damn, the game left ... heavy heart (heavy heart)

/ The streets left ... heavy heart (heart) ... gave this hustle everything" (Meek Mill)

*

Rechercher. To search. To look again. Relook. To search is an act of repetition. To search is to to research. Linearity be damned. Enter co-occurence. Re-enter co-occurence. Pre-enter co-occurence.

*

Next logical step landed on the landing where passion would descend. Go instairs away from heaven but back into the earth. Find its roots in the core. Leave behind the souls and spirits ascending. Reasonably vacate the streets. Deathless but beyond living as living is so seen.

*

"Deathless ... Left for dead in the streets / Whatever happens, whatever happened" (Ibeyi)

"a nigga gotta pay the fucking rent" (Tupac)

"what makes symmetry nonsense" (Virginia Woolf - the Waves)

*

Remote. By remoteness, controlled. Phantoms lead the way (present and past tense). something sticks. Gets wrapped around a thought. This is suspicion.

Aliens and astronauts have eyes that are not to be believed. Tuesday came before Monday. As Tuesday once again will come after Monday but less distance put between the two yet meanwhile, some pupils would feel free to float away. Some irises would travel above rainbows then come down containing different mysteries.

These eyes, now hard as hell, fancy new fancies. Or hard as hail, rain, pour out something else of a different composure. A different purpose. Containing a fancy **for** another identity. An active attraction streaming into the darkest of matters.

*

Ghosts are not invisible but differently sensed.

*

Where lights are directly above, where the lights are brightest and floor freshly waxed, the shadows fade into reflections. What hour is it in the wake of the florescent sun? The false light on skin, touching eyes, brings neither wakefulness nor enlightenment. It's too late for a revelation right now. This is the before. Something has yet to exist. A haunting feeling comes over and breaks bread. Joins in on breaktime. Becomes coffee. Eats alongside some worn out ideas.

*

The night might be black. Might be bright. Could be full moon in Scorpio. Could be full moon in Sagittarius. If only eyes filmed as opposed to filled. It is bright. Tasks asked for one to go out. To exit into the cold. Might be full moon in Capricorn or Aquarius. The seasons waver. The moon is but one face that occurs. Tasks recur and recur. It is cold. It is bright. It might be full moon in Pisces. Life is committed to tasks and misery. The schedule domesticates the traces of daydreams happening and happening again in the night. Thoughts walking out of step among the phrases hanging in the air of the night. Cold. Inherited from the game. It is cold. It is basketball season. It is hockey season. It is football season. It is holiday season. It is not Cancer nor Leo but the moon is full. It is sweeps season. The episodes are new. Commercials are breaking somewhere. Commercials have broken the stream of songs in the headphones. It is full moon in Taurus. The horoscope reads, "In love, tensions are pointless. It's going to be a beautiful day, with no unpleasant events."

*

Outlines and underlays. Not for nothing, come to find out, what had happened wasn't how it was. Not even how thinking ahead thought it would go.

*

Please add flavor packet after microwaving soup. It is hot. The tongue is sensitive. This bit of flesh is weak. The rest of the flesh feels no such way. Is not susceptible to skin hunger. No pangs for touch. Averse to hugs and embrace but still longing for love if love can accept the terms and agreements. Follow the instructions. Agree to some fine print.

*

"... write off hospitality ... enough hassle / enough stress ... everything doesn't start again until tomorrow" (Kristín Svava Tómasdóttir - Stormwarning)

*

Let it go. Just lost a lot of words. Thoughts disappeared. Made a mistake and now it's gone. No backup. Nothing to revert to. That was the before that occurred. There is no return. Whatever survived will be understood later on but there's no welcome for the stresses of trying to remember what once was constructed. Those structures that were assembled, crumbled. Leave it be. Those buildings weren't memories yet. Those phrases weren't even built as far as the world is concerned. What happened in one's head is for one alone on this occasion.

*

"Disciplinarians thrive under chaos." (Zane - Nervous)

*

Routine and banality. More of same. Scheduled. Eat, sleep. Consider, reconsider. Be nervous. Anxious. Start again at the end. After a break. Embrace the gap. Let the space rub up against the mind's skin. Let distance become a tactile thought. A pinch. A kiss. A lover without any sense of charm.

"The person that loves the least, controls the relationship." (Zane - Total Eclipse of the Heart)

Whomever and whatever. Even the inanimate have a sense of love that can applied to it if somebody is willing to apply it. Some folks have installed failsafe romanticism to push back against all odds.

"this is how trauma learns to behave." (Marwa Helal - Invasive Species)

*

Is this happening in real time? How does the surreal differ from this? How does the hyperreal give credit to this? Who invited the magical real? Why did folks forget about the marvelous real?

In what approach to the real do daydreams appear? Is there room for a simulation or only acceleration?

Is there room for vacillation or in this vortex is there only further in and inward no back and forth? What good is being a ghost if one must remain to weather the storm minus the ability to feel the rain? Can't smell the flowers either wherever weeds grow tall enough to be mistaken for plants such as those. Definitions are malleable. Lexicons keep growing. Voyages outward are rewarded with more vocabulary but a vocabulary does **have way,** a **tendency,** to do a person in or so **some** corny dead white poet thought.

*

Bus stops and bus rides. Commute. No communion.

More opportunities for the journey inside. Downside. To talk would be a trip outside, upside. Sides and stairs in / out, up / down.

Apron strings and coattails. Been **let** down before, still there is the afterwards. Is afterwards into? Towards or outwards? What direction is after heading? What's on after's mind? What was before expecting? Here is confused. There already always gave up while the submitting was good. Gave in when the surrendering was giving good offers for giving up. Haunting has learned to haggle. Ghosts are great debators. Spectres on the other hand have sticky fingers. Pickpocket while nostalgia starts setting in – scared and melancholy. Grave robbers don't require a body, death is ever near. Aliens abduct and stories are rarely taken seriously.

*

"the one true love is settling / a score / peeling back the skin reveals no meaning ... beautiful, but insincere / new heaven, new earth" (elvis depressedly)

*

Is it Thursday? If it is, is it time for a throwback? Yesterday's drama is just as fresh as today's. In reference to other times, today enjoys its position of difference while savoring the similarity. The dissonance is real.

*

Some thoughts will never get what is deserved. Never get what it has coming. Ideas find the slim spaces, slide in and hide out, reside, live happily ever after.

Once upon a time, things were different. Sense was never made but existed. Occurred. This was not always these pieces. Was not broken.

Wasted a lot of time. Lived life calling for a calling, got no replies. Got caught up in the sound of wishes. Tasted prayers. Could've sworn that miracles had an odor that hung in the air. Considered hanging one way to reach blessings. Get closer to God. Was happier than those words would relay. Thought and talk never went to therapy to get the counseling needed to communicate. Come to an agreement. But love is the air. That shit stays hanging around. Ain't got nowhere to go but don't like hanging out. Sends a text. Makes no plans. Considers the span and expanse of a kiss.

*

"Still thirsty determined and motivated ... Real niggas ain't never outdated." (E-40)

*

Keeping that same energy, different desire but the romance is real. Exists somewhere. Is broken. The broken blade is the Negro. Time to complete each other or be completed. Repaired.

Step into a notion. Feel a feeling. Reverse roles. Role play. Whatever it takes.

*

One can leave the hood but the hood never leaves one alone. One always has the hood as a running partner. The hood has heart. The hood has a heart. A sidekick for tragedy, comedy, or romance. Staves off a bit of loneliness. Keeps neediness at bay while respecting the game. Got to have goals. Got to play to win. Work for victory.

*

The shadow of flesh casts how deep and far / a landscape of perspective? / how round / a circumference enough to fit the living / world does a single life turning to its labor spin? (Ed Roberson - Eclogue)

*

"Inherent in all of this? Self-deceit. The notion that storms to be narrated are external. Rich atmospheres. Human beings struggle against the elements or against other beings, as if the elements and the enemies weren't also —and especially— internal." (Luisa Valenzuela - Dark Desires and the Others)

*

The hood embodies this. The ghetto is here. Beyond inscapes. Inward. Inside.

*

"inscape, the distinctive design that constitutes individual identity. This identity is not static but dynamic. Each being in the universe 'selves,' that is, enacts its identity." (Stephen Greenblatt on Gerard Manley Hopkins)

*

Universe: "the aggregate of all humanity's consciously apprehended and communicated (to self or others) Experiences." (Buckminster Fuller)

*

Note to self: Places are named. Certain times too as in noon, midnight, morning, afternoon, evening but not the minute, save for quarter past and to and half. Be more attune to time. Less to place.

*

A note found. Used as a bookmark. Something leftover from a trip. An envelope that once contained a name. A little thing the folks did at readings. Something different. Seen a lot now. This was a change.

Note reads: a rising and overflowing of a body of water.

But, the idea of a flood of which this note was defining as everybody got a disaster, no, instead thoughts go to "et" and ampersand and all the ways to draw "and" more so than to write it. And becomes its own geography. A landscape of an idea.

Not every idea gets a sign. Not so many to be sure. Not signs that aren't words but pictures. Is there always more to come? Something in addition to? Many times one in and of the same hoped so. One still does. One will. Is willed to.

Identity feels very addentity. Maybe &entity.

*

"a drone / Bouncing off a satellite / Crushin' the last lone American night / This is radio nowhere, is there / anybody alive out there?" (Bruce Springsteen)

Never forgive the hour of the day but forget how time passes. Ask a song for some company. Beg for help with these tasks. Try to unbecome the drudgery.

Channels change. Turn into playlists. Are streamed in. Buffer in the edges of the building, are lost in the elevator. Some of the cleaning is accompanied by silence. Got to remember to download something for these spaces. For the jobs that send one to sites where signals go incommunicado.

Two dead parents won't text here anymore. An ex sometimes does. The best of the exes won't. Friends are asleep or drunk. Everybody is in a better place. Have somebody else for communication.

Loneliness suggests it's time to go back to scrolling. Work suggests it's time to get back to work.

*

When is this? When is here? In what moment is the occurring? How is existence doing these days? Or is it nights?

What kind of range does this have, own, occupy? Is this free-range or cage free. There is no ethical occurring under existing.

*

What are daydreams made of? Sensations are set free while something else slips in? What else? Hope? Hope is a broken blade. Hope snapped off the handle. Couldn't get through the tasks at hand. Hard to handle comes to mind and nobody needs that. Nobody asked for that. Waves of emotion are at low tide for now. The swell has subsided. It's the tough time when sights say what needs to be thought about.

This is no time to sit down and talk. Interior dialogue is put on pause. Is broken. This negro is broke if not broken. Not about losing a job just yet but hope any day now will be soon.

*

Grew up on the grind. Part of the game is the work. Approaching is an act. Can't get nowhere waiting. Well, except to the after. The after don't care none about how anybody arrived nor approached it.

In the end, it's always darkest before the after so work done in the dark must one day come to light.

The hustle reveals itself. The jig is up. The con comes crumbling down. Inward and instairs of self. Closer to the core. To the heart or to the gut? Pick a poison.

*

Back in day was a mix of too many everythings. The radio was too many streams beelining into ears. Didn't quite know what to turn on and what to turn off. Jazz was out though. How were those baby ears programmed? How was a sense of taste in music crafted? Good and bad through the ears. What within earshot was so responsible for thoughts and feelings to come? Now, when taste is questioned how many ways can one front? Try to play it cool when tucked inside is:

"How to sell a contradiction ... Red, gold, and green, red, gold, and green ... love was an addiction ... love is strong ... survival (survival) ... without conviction" (Culture Club)

Took the important parts to heart. Left gaps where gaps felt natural.

*

"In a big country dreams stay ... a lover's voice fires the mountainside / Stay alive" (Big Country)

*

Learned to listen less obviously. All pleasures are guilty now. Pleasure stands accused of crimes against before.

*

"Measure time in leisure time and greed" (Hurray for the Riff Raff)

*

On break where "the street-talk birdcall of sucked teeth" (Ed Roberson) is abundant. It's hoops time of the year and it's never not hip-hop time of the year. Trap, mumble, and throwbacks.

And it's reggaeton and soul. And it's a whole lot of signifying and hating. And that new Dolemite shit just dropped. And this nigga dissed that one. And the breakroom is lit.

"Yo, from the first to the last of it, delivery is passionate / The whole and not the half of it, vocab and not the math of it" (Black Star)

Keep flipping the narrative. Deepening the debate. Trying to make a point even if ain't nobody staying on topic. Switch it up till there's something worth wasting time discussing. Bums and trash ain't trying to have no space at lunch. That can be talked about on the clock. Let the boss pay for basura. That's what a janitor gets paid to do. Maintenance deals with the garbage but on break, it's back to being a free agent again. No tasks at hand but to get back on time or close enough. Use all the grace period. Push freedom to its limit. Talk ain't cheap. It got a price. Willing to pay the cost if it means not having to listen to the boss. HNIC ain't shit. Another punk playing with some fakeass proximity to the real pros. Worked up now keeping other niggas down. Sold out for what? For who? That ain't the way of the hood. It's either about the community or sole proprietor. No money going back into certain back pockets. Even worse, time is life. Can't be out here losing a life for somebody else's bank account when ain't nobody trying to take into account another's life.

Changed views as more of the world started to come into focus. Seen more shit and less and less of the soil from which this nigga grew.

Thought there was a shared before but that don't mean nothing even if it did occur. The after will separate the wheat from the chaff. The wheat from the tares. All skin folk ain't kinfolk. Some lessons take a lifetime to learn. Some lives take too much time learning the same lessons again and again.

*

Too late to scream "peace." Shit already been started. How anybody supposed to forget any trespasses? When a line has been crossed, forgiveness is the last task on the list and it ain't never gonna be completed. There's some to-do type shit that ain't going to ever be done but it has been taken note of, acknowledged, ignored. Fuck that shit but ain't no sense in complaining about it. Keep on keeping on. Accept no apologies from oppressors. Not all enemies are oppressors. That distinction needs to be made clear. Some treaties are possible. The hood accepts an armistice. The ghetto survived on detente days. But oppressors will always push the envelope, break boundaries, ask for more, give less, and erase any histories that reject the official story. History was written not by the winners but by those who want to see to it that somebody else will continue to lose. Even better, don't fight back.

*

"The day tomorrow will be worse but that does not mean that the day today is not bad." (Birta Lif Kristindóttir - meteorologist)

*

What's in the cards? What's been pulled? Another fool? A joke on the querent once again?

*

"just a mirror in the dark / Seeking up a long lost look" (Twin Shadow)

*

Looking for answers anywhere at this point. The angels' lips are sealed. The phantoms took off on ghost ships. The poltergeists inhabit ghost towns. All the intelligence around here feels very artificial. All the advice is based on an algorithm. The androids are pulling the strings while niggas are left here to toe the line.

*

Been working on being on the level. Trying to stay narrow if not straight. Always got a bit of a con brewing. Thief thoughts are the first love. Don't steal except when broke these days. Turns out, 4 out of 5 days...

*

"no better half can satisfy / A wasted alibi" (Cautious Clay)

*

Try to think about better times. Other lives. Another before of which this is the after. Worked hard for somebody else. Having somebody around made somethings more clear. Made work feel less a waste. Worked more. Lost a life into a job. Lost it into lies. And yet still miss something about those times.

*

Been losing faith and religion.

"No longer yearn to be gentle and pure and sweet / Not intimidating yet sure" (Vagabon)

Not the same person who applied for the job.

Summertime came. Wintertime went. Fall was before. Spring was after. The thaw broke the ice and gave up secrets that the air wasn't meant to hear. The breeze spread the word all over the skin. Skin crawled but couldn't get away. Been holding a grudge ever since. No matter how fresh the air is, it is always unclean. Can't trust a breeze by any name - Adriatic, Bora, Mistral, Sirocco, Tramuntana, nor Levanter. Pirates have an uneasy understanding with the atmosphere. Prayers and preparation can fail. Gods will renege at any time. Conditions change quickly. Terms are up for adjusting.

All agreements hold as much weight as trying to talk to the lightning. But got to keep on moving. Two tears in a bucket.

Meditation just don't hit the same way it used to. Try to breathe. Stay rightminded. Gentle has been the goal. Fuse is shorter than should be admitted to.

*

"Don't get dead." (Chester Himes - Cotton Comes to Harlem)

*

It's a chore to not pop off. Retorts are on tap. Volume is set to increase. People want to blame emotions but its reason that conjures up the anger. Untruths and inequality in the microcosm. Can't take it. Can't get canned either. And the schedule is too good to let go. Giving up the good for the great has ended up much worse too many times.

*

Get dead. Create one's own ending. Assemble the last. Forget about the before and it's darkness always already around. Ready-made depths around even in an oasis of light, two floors of retail at a standstill, lack of customers. Just workers. Just work. Just...

*

There are lots of ways to get dead whether one is on the up and up or a petty sneak-thief. Seen folks leave this world lots of different ways. A few lost while doing a job. A legit gig. Stocking shelves. Here. Heart attacks and strokes. Boxer. Sent to the glue factory for supporting the system.

*

Been waiting one long cotton-picking minute for things to get better.

*

"Oh, happy day

(oh, happy day)

Oh, happy day

(oh, happy day)

When jesus washed

(when jesus washed)" (Edwin Hawkins)

*

"Thank God for squares." (Chester Himes - Cotton Comes to Harlem)

*

The company store. Half working and half window shopping. All those illuminati videos can't stave off looking for a good deal. Some people in hell might want ice water but in this particular hell, big screen TVs are preferable.

*

Double talk doing overtime. Never-ending revisions to policies and protocols. Raises reduced. Holiday pay removed. Sick pay eliminated. Less latenesses / absences. Lateness, itself, redefined. Benefits renegotiated. Less coming this way. More going that way. Every day is a losing proposition.

*

Misunderstandings happen. Apologies don't always follow. Agree to disagree. Disagree to agree. Maybe nobody was wrong. Maybe both are incorrect.

Will still lose sleep over situation regardless. Arguments live a second, third, fourth, etc life in the quiet moments. In the dead of the night. When dreams are impossible, only thing left is thinking. The subconscious sent back to the bench.

*

"Perhaps [this] 'no hope' therapy is a little ridiculous; never hope, to avoid disappointment; consider [oneself] dead, to keep from dying." (Adolfo Bioy Casares - The Invention of Morel)

*

Yellow from regret. Pale is a bit out of the question. At a loss of color as regrets are becoming fears. There are no conclusions. The coda just gives the after time to better prepare. The after never loses. The after is undefeated but before doesn't enjoy talking about it.

*

Spend nights trying to unexplore visits to the places only a few go. Those parts of the city that kids aren't meant to be in while watching parents. Observing what adulthood can become. Spend time away from the self. This place is its own sort of ward for the sorts of folks who chose to work this shift doing this shit.

*

"tho' anatomy is not a butcher knife / one can use its keen edge to / lop off / branches, out-croppins" (Stephen Jonas)

*

Ted Joans was dying. Ted Joans is dead. Objective chance remains. Surrealism is (in) the afterlife.

*

Objective chance is "an active synthesis of the subjective and the objective," (Michel Carrouges)

"The form of the manifestation of external necessity that finds its way to the subconscious." (André Breton)

*

Night terrors. Night terrors. Daydreams daydreams. Switched. Who took whose place? Up all night daydreaming. Stuck in bed beside the midday sun paralyzed by night terrors.

*

"Believe in this. Young apple seeds, / In blue skies, radiating young breast, / Not in blue-suited insects, / Infesting society's garments." (Bob Kaufman)

*

There are no blue skies here. There are elsewhere. In another when there are skies of different hues. Can't see the sky anyway here beneath this roof.

*

"Different stretch of road, new somethin to see / Every state on the map, a different somethin to eat / Daps and handshakes, it meant nuttin for real / Everybody makin a Killin ... showin no feelins / Walkin off collectin pay, it's the way of the world / Can't change it" (Nappy Roots)

*

What kind of friends are possible under capitalism? Niggas out here trying to get paid can't be trusted. Rats and snitches trying to get ahead but ain't getting shit. Tattletales and temper tantrums. Somebody is being sold out right now as these thoughts come to mind. Turn one against the other without even pretending to make promises.

*

"coming from a long bloodline of trauma ... poisoned the well / Distorted self image ... set up to fail ... / the real gon' prevail, nigga" (J Cole)

*

Trying to consider common knowledge. Reconsidering common sense. Long nights watching customers till the doors close then again when doors open up 6 hours later. 6 hours away from the larger world. The microcosm comes with its own rules. Who built this world? Who created the other one? Worker and patrons live in different dimensions that crossover at the nexus of the product. Nameless to the world. Just get the trash. Push the broom. It's better this way. It wasn't the dream but it works.

*

It doesn't work. It is broken.

*

"Six million ways to die / Choose one" (Cutty Ranks)

*

What have all those classrooms ever done for anybody here? College kids shopping. Was a college kid too. Started here as a college (not quite) kid. Another round of classes. Older. Different point of view. The perspective that comes with the fracturing of narratives. Thanks for all those lessons. Learned how to push through. Push on knowing help never comes when it's needed. Read the wrong stuff too early and the right shit too late. Self-reliant upon self told lies taken from misunderstandings. So how does one end up here? The before is a story no longer in favor of being told. Everybody has a story. Call it a legacy no matter where one lands. The world keeps spinning and the system grinds folks to dust. Chalk dust and cracked slate. Words were somewhere. Words are somewhere else now alongside other ways to learn. Back to the roots. What used to be said on those stoops? Outlandish for the outsiders.

*

"When American life is most American it is apt to be most theatrical." (Ralph Ellison - Shadow and Act)

*

Everyday is a show. The puffy-shirt pirates and the folks beneath the Stetsons beside the saguaro are just movies now. Just books. Just songs. But, the gangstas and the do-gooders exist and coincide / collide everyday. Everybody has necessities. The store provides those. Different walks of life walk into one another.

*

"that which cannot gain authority from tradition may borrow it" (Ralph Ellison - Shadow and Act)

*

Hand to phone. Against the rules. Hidden up in the cut. The boonies of salesfloor trying to keep up on the news and the gossip. Seeing something to get upset about. The feed is always good for that. The influencers flex the falsest influence or the truest. Sincerity is hard to read on the screen on borrowed time.

*

The phone is made of masks. The screen breaks but the masks remain. Reputations were made and are less ephemeral than in olden days. The before isn't before anymore.

*

"Money's awfully nice to have. In fact, all things considered ... it's even worth the price." (Nella Larsen - Passing)

*

Do what one got to do find a little happiness. It's what the angels would want. It's why some angels fall. Some angels fell in love with the ways of this world. Then rewrote those ways.

*

"The sky, lazily disdaining to pursue / The setting sun, too indolent to hold / A lengthened tournament for flashing gold, / Passively darkens" (Jean Toomer - Georgia Dusk)

*

But the dark is not passive. Actively removing light but not fully. Room is left for stars. Room is left for the moon. City lights pollute the potential of the night and nothing is as bright nor as dark as it could be elsewhere. But this is all a process, a slow one, that began with the shadows of the dawn and the shortened shade of high noon. Darkness didn't wait but creeping back towards its takeover. And the night is filled with the sounds of the bars and clubs, folks catching up on TV, snoring, and the ignored people of the last shift. The unseen. Or at least the lesser seen. The less acknowledged. The folks who lose rest and relaxation to get normal things done. Waiting for banks and laundromats to open. Up for a trim. Up for shopping. Staying up. Knowing that night is never too far behind.

*

The night is spent wishing. That's what the stars charge those for being up in those hours, occupying those times. Certain hours same as certain places are for certain beings. Give to the night what is the night's. Give the ghosts and aliens some breathing room. Give the vermin some freedom from being seen as a scourge. As eyes adjust, spirits are already well underway upon the hauntings that need to be done. Skin gets ready for the chill. Might desire other skin. Might only have eyes for blankets. The bed might be the apple of the eye. The constellations conspire to say which people prefer which company. The psychoanalysts got together and made other decisions. Either way, real people can be real archetypes too. Can enter into themes. Can be a symbol for something else. Martyred before death.

*

Don't gotta a whole lotta love left. Pinching pennies squeezed the love out of life. Trying to save a little for somebody else but it's getting hard. The best things in life might be free but who has the free time to go get whatever those things are? Ain't even got time to smile anymore.

*

Got a pot to piss in. Ain't got a whole lot of beer to make the piss though. Ain't got too much coffee either. Ain't got a refrigerator that's full. Ain't got nothing in the cabinet but realities that don't go well together. It ain't a meal.

*

Hand over fist. Tooth and nail. Can't fight no more. Ain't nothing worth all that fuss. Nothing ever changes in the right ways. The deck is stacked and the reading ain't never been pleasant. Ain't even fair.

*

Fireflies and lightning bugs. Mosquitoes filling up the outside. In here the seasons don't change. In here it ain't summer. It's the 4th of July plates and napkins and that's about it. It's Christmas but it ain't winter. It ain't even holiday season just the busy time. School didn't prepare anybody for what comes next. Didn't warn anybody about the end of weekends and summer vacations and hard work paying off.

*

The pirates left treasures for archeologists to salvage. Deep sea divers bringing up memories that couldn't be taken down to the depths of the next world. Some days are spent attempting to salvage something from another sense of self. But selves rust, rot, and erode. Some selves were thrown overboard. Walked the plank. Some were mutineers. Some weren't pulling any weight. Some selves were merely stowaways.

*

Prefer the synthetic to the artificial. Prefer the artificial to be synthetic. Prefer the natural to be synthetic too. Pro synthesis. Anything to unite against chance. Or to unite into a more singular subjective chance of mutual sensings. Shared sensibilities. A sentimentality of togetherness.

*

A love letter is not a love story. A ghost story is not a ghost letter. Letters don't need plots just characters. A letter is too direct for all that. Even a letter that has disappeared, was written and is gone now but exists in the memory of the writer who was direct and directly lives on to correspond with the writer. The deleted text is never really deleted. What does a story do but rearrange the details and as such misdirects. Leaves one waiting for more, hopeful. The letter can state everything up front or hold off the request until the end. Rhetoric evades no writing not even writing to oneself. But the desires for the words shifts the styling, the aesthetics. Story is too stifling. Suspense and twists. Conflict and conclusion. Action in and of itself. Exposition. What if all anybody needs is a good long note?

*

A love note written after being ghosted. One last response. Gone but not forgotten.

*

Stockpiled sentimentality since childhood. Couldn't use it then but now could be the time. Could be the place. Some comfort when it is darkest. Something from before. Something that is not broken but for somebody who might be – for whatever that means. Why do people say that? How horrible and rarely true. **Willing to** say it's a possibility for somebody but who? Who is broken? How? Who put the effort into that breakage?

Who created rifts? Pressed a valley into a place begging for a mountaintop?

By those gaps may another greatness be reframed.

*

Vanity among those without much of anything is an ars poetica against humility. Pride can be lovely in the lowest of places. Hubris in the hardest times is an act of self-love. It's not easy keeping up the affection for oneself when the world is working against the inscapes.

Down in those imaginary, figurative, and metaphorical dumps. Or in those real dumps or near the very real dumpsters where nobody's trash is anybody else's treasure. Where somebody knows trash when it's been cleaned up. Where somebody knows treasure when it's been seen in the movies. Where outside is littered with the remnants of stories unheard / unseen but sensed. Somebody had pizza. Somebody bought new shoes. Somebody changed the oil. Somebody installed a new car seat. Can understand on some level what occurred. Can sense the before. Is left to clean up the liminal limits of the after.

*

"got to find a way to bring some lovin' here today" (Marvin Gaye)

*

"Judgments are not at all reflections ... habits prompt ... judgments more than ... tastes do. And how can [one] tell a taste from a habit, an inclination from a subjection?" (Anne Garréta - Not One Day)

*

Used to enjoy a run. Knees feel different more recently. The slow walk instairs and outstairs doesn't help. The steps through the building don't do what those steps outside did. It's all exercise that much is true. Calories burned. But that necessity of movement as dictated by the task takes away the sensation that should come from the going. The pacing is all anxiety whereas the run brought calmness or an answer to questions rattling around. It was time to investigate. This walking is more about observing. Moving isn't as habitual as one thinks. One foot in front of the other but what about the rest of the body?

*

Personally is the only way to take anything. Personal is all anybody is even publically. Getting carried away is just another way to travel. From mood to mood is no short trip and is filled with layovers in other feelings. Delays on the runways of emotions. Through time.

Through space. Through the ideas not yet fully explained. Paranormal paranoia transgresses upon the purity of sadness.

*

The grind never stops. One is ground down. Honed. Waves break upon the self. Endlessly. The grind varies. High and low tides. Tidal waves. The pounding differs but continues. Where is a break from the breaking? A new day is necessary. A day to break what the night brought.

*

Poker and spades. Talking across the board. The game and the job, the play and the work work through codes. Words have hidden values. Say more than said. Numerology, Kabbalah, and the 5 Percenters can confirm this. Those who know know and those who know don't say. Codes take time to get. Deciphering comes alone. No assistance.

*

Wish for more. Accept less. Streams of music coming in taking chances on stations instead of playlists. Maybe a program can make better choices than the listener can. Just want something random but not too random. Planned chaos. A little disarray kept inside designated boundaries. Keep the probability down.

*

The gum lost its flavor now all that remains is the texture. A touch inside a mouth and the ghost of a taste. Spit yearns for more than a memory.

*

This place ain't nothing but a fancy coffin. Would rather be cremated. Elevators add to the sensation of a crypt. Hidden staircases remind one of catacombs. Lockers are a mausoleum of valuables.

*

"Americans love being conned ... if the style is both grand and entertaining." (Ishmael Reed - Yellow Back Radio Broke-down)

*

Barely functioning. Can't keep living up to this lifestyle. The body doesn't feel the way it once did. Fatigue is a stronger pull than before.

Work, sleep, work. Annoyance of messages to answer. Emails to respond to. Comments. Too many comments on posts that don't require any. Eat. Maybe eat too much for whatever that means. Need to go back to the gym for whatever need means. Why bother? Alone in health or alone in sickness is all the same alone.

Didn't have the drinks to get here. Didn't have the weed to get right. Didn't have the pills to set the back straight. Neither body nor mind are ever ready for the night anymore.

Unhappy with what's at hand. Not too much different on the outside. Death is always around. Cafés are cemeteries waiting to happen. The bar is graveyard whether it's packed or it's dead.

*

Put on a happyish face. Make the next joke. That's part of the job too. A part that only oneself can add and only oneself keep oneself to. Don't be the reason for lowering the total morale. Don't take a different approach to what the company and the managers do too well. Don't nobody need that.

Be back in bed soon enough. Can consider a drink then. Can think about weed in whatever form is available. Terminal velocity return to a frown.

Don't get dead. More to go. It's a marathon not a track meet. Anything to alleviate the waves.

*

"one nation under hell" (Pure Hell)

*

Two parents down. No more to go. Could use one more vice while it's getting down to the wire. Is love finished?

*

What's that texture? That's the texture of a familiar if not similar moment. Skin upon skin. Dap. Pound. A greeting. One-arm around the back. In it together.

*

"timeless children ... the news lately ... were sad? / Shot, that's on the pass / All the dreams were flying / All the love was dying / Earth was coming fast" (Death)

"what bitter Americana" (Ishmael Reed - Yellow Back Broke-Down Radio)

*

Fuck money. Would be nice to work for something else for a change.

*

Time travelers and cryptids. A world of mysteries. Reptilians, walk-ins, indigo children. Chemtrails. Late night radio and podcasts trying to tell the truth about the shadows.

Comic books aren't very comedic anymore. The funny pages are deadly serious now.

Showboats and hotshots. Superpowers and special abilities. Paranormal and supernatural. Secret identities. Fuck government names. Villains and vigilantes. Arch-enemies. Sibling rivalries. Families torn apart. Orphans and adoptees.

Symbols. Signs. Sigils.

*

Gris-gris, talismans, and totems. Spirits, blessings, tributes, and hexes. Real life rituals and beliefs.

Superstitions are for sports teams trying to make it to the big game. For theater to be more dramatic.

For neurotic kids to better blend in on the schoolyard.

*

Holidays are coming up and there ain't no wishbones for vegans.

The holidays are gone and so are the wishes. Gotta wait for a birthday now.

*

"Don't cook tonight, call Chicken Delight" and Bojangles Famous Chicken 'n' Biscuits occupied small spots in childhood. What's taking those places in adulthood? Never get the Proustian from hipster tofu but still looking for that spot that makes bean curd the way it was made back in the day on the old block, round the way when going vegetarian wasn't nothing Black folks would do. Give up pork? Maybe, everybody got Muslims in the family. Some, Rastas was on that Ital lifestyle but not no normal regular Black niggas. This is what happens when folks get too uppity. Now, good food ain't good enough? What did chicken do?

Suffering is growing away from old joys and not getting new ones. Learned to cook. Went pro. Made lots of people happy. Mostly white folks with some money to burn and dietary issues, not necessarily ethical ones. But, anybody can find a way to be self-righteous. Maybe even this is. There's no way nirvana is coming any time soon. Gonna stay trying. Gonna die guiding. Hoping this help ain't a detour. Praying against the waylay.

Made mistakes. Misunderstood books and didn't take on any teachers.

There will be mangoes. There will be yucca. Arroz con gandules will be jollof rice back where Spanish niggas was stolen from. There will be Bustelo and tostones to press to the tongue to try to bring back the neighborhood and person that are no longer here.

*

"went back...city was gone / There was no train station...downtown...had disappeared...favorite places...had been pulled down" (Sleepy John Estes)

*

Sometimes even city niggas can feel the country in something between the bones. In the connective tissue and the disconnection of epigenetics. The land and the sea sing choruses in the soul. Dirt, mud, and soil. Sun, sweat, earth, and birth. Ain't no forgetting roots no matter how far down. Grandfolks and further back and further back. There's country everywhere. Land of Jibaro, slaves, and sharecroppers. Caribbean, Creole, Southern. Out west. But won't never be no clown at a rodeo. Won't drive cattle and can't sing a few bars with Hank Sr. Can't sing with the black folks who done shown Sr those chords either.

Might not know anything about the reaping but sooner or later, the sowing comes.

*

"the sun no longer quantified / by strange calendrical posses / but becomes / balletic differential / which ceases to quarrel / with the magic of fragment as schism" (Will Alexander - Inside the Ghost Volcano)

*

Infested and infected by words. Unloved by words. Uncared for by words. Disconnected by language. Solitary. Banished. Confined by having nothing else to say and having already said too much.

*

"Which one will it be? Time alone will tell ... writing this diary can perhaps provide the answer; it may even help produce the right future." (Adolfo Bioy Casares - the Invention of Morel)

*

Can oversleep but can't really overwake. Well, maybe be overwoke but that's something else completely. Could one enter wakefulness too awake, too amped? Too psyched? There are people who are a little too much for just getting out of bed.

Here's where one gets to learn about envy. It's been slow risings more recently. What was lost in the waking? How much was wasted in the getting to the going? No time is ever really one's own. It's all owed to somebody or something else so hoarding time is nigh impossible. Creditors will come along any time now. Now when now is least expected. Render unto whenever whatever is whenever's and unto the self whatever is leftover. Second-hand time and thriftstore space will have to do. Vintage memories will go up in value. Antique daydreams will be worth more than **what was** lost while waiting for a good deal. Buy low and sell high. Flip every thought.

*

Can't point to a point of view. Can't pinpoint a perspective to give to anybody else. Subjectivity seems closer to lies sometimes. There's always another story or it didn't happen.

*

Wonder what really made **it** to the permanent record. What was worth recording in the eyes of the **school?**

*

The sentence as a flame of phrases is not an image. All one has in some sort of reality is the idea to revisit. To push into oneself. To put into a mental rendering of bodily contingencies as understood through dueling sensibilities of before and those less further removed befores. What earthly experiences are getting in the way of other experiences? What borders between image and idea must be moved for a better sentimentality?

*

"How to unknot the thread of desire. Dream up nights. Wander again among the shadows." (Anne Garréta - Not One Day)

*

How many airports is it now where there was no good-bye? How many trains arrived to the lack of hello? Don't ever want to resist an intimate sensation. Desire memories with high watermarks but instead am left to cry over the spilled milk of the mundane even when the routine itself has been challenged. Change of pace and place but the same outcomes. The inscapes are too strong too crumble under the waves. Or broken is the structure. But not further broken. Shattered is its own pattern. The scattering has a rhythm it keeps to itself and among its pieces.

Yet, don't let this devalue what never had any value. Let nothingness be cherished for simply being itself.

*

The wee hours are worse than the big ones. Those ones, twos, threes of the AM bring on the pressure of time management but also of moods. Too much time alone to think. Too many songs heard. Too much conversation or too little. One break down and lunch never really satisfies the way a meal should. Getting closer to the end, dominoes of emotions get going around the place. Top down and down back up. Machines act up. Clogs in hoses. Batteries drain faster than expected. Garbage compactor is clogged. Cardboard baler needs more attention to keep its door closed. The handheld scanners can't seem to locate and connect to the printers. The buttons are sticking on the electric lifts and pallet jacks. At least the escalator is working. And the freight elevator might be fucked again but the passenger elevators are OK for now.

*

Maybe it's been a long time away from home. Maybe thoughts of going home to oneself are starting to flood in. Thinking of auto-eroticism. Not thinking about anybody here. Thinking of nothing real. Nobody in particular but sometimes those come in. Would prefer romance but that's not the pirate way. That's a desperadon't. The angels approve. The androids don't care. Androids never care. Do the ghosts remember romance more than sex? The aliens know a good time when eyes can't be believed.

The books and the songs didn't agree on what to want. Desire was spilt between the literary and lyrics. Then comedy also comes. It's gotta all be funny. One must imagine confusion as happiness.

*

Affection is absurdity. Is collaboration a form of resistance? Together can create a wall. A barricade. That's the word used in Les Misérables and who isn't miserable enough for a bit of revolution?

*

If all goes well, the pirates are willing participants in whatever the elements want to do. The elements aren't the enemy. Desire is. The need to go. The need to stay. The need to keep. The elements don't care about these desires. The outside and inside rarely agree unless the outside is on the same page as the inside. If the outside isn't an obstacle, it's a comrade.

The elements, the metals tucked into the earth didn't ask to be uncovered. Had no say in becoming valuable as parts nor as decoration. Didn't ask the world to make slaves to dig into it.

A desire for something sweet. A sweet tooth bites into the hands of involuntary workers.

Can't figure out how to be both the villain and cooperative. But then again pirates ain't exactly about redistributing the wealth either. There's a whole lot of holding on there too. But reading the wind is something. Some performers can't even take the temperature of a room and complain about hitting rock bottom. Then even more so about how much the bottom can give.

It's not an antihero's world nor an antipoet's but there's a reason to take up an opposite perspective. Don't worry about middles. Not yet. Moderation as a game plan can't lead to victory here on earth but in heaven maybe, in terms of rebirth, probably, in limbo definitely. But this is the antiworld, the before. The real world will be here in the after. It is dark but not darkest. The moon is full. The shapes are shifting. The wolves will pounce. The stars said this. Those who know, knew this. Predicted it even if the future is flexible.

*

Don't lose the thread not when the sewing is going so well. Rips are being stitched and thus accentuated in another way.

Wait, do holes feel lonely? Stop. Drop that needle.

*

Where on earth is heaven? Where'd the angels go? Where do earthbound spirits long to call home?

*

Don't have a stutter so to speak but when words aren't ready to come out, there's some skipping of the record. Thoughts buffer. Nerves can't connect to tongue. Tongue refuses the connection. Been burned before. That pizza, that coffee, that kiss, that mispronunciation. Too hot to handle sometimes. Even there, letting that song come along could burn the mouth if it gets out. There's nothing cool about that. Gotta stay cool. Can't be a cornball out in these streets. Out in any streets. Or indoors, in these walls made up of folks who came in off those streets. Same streets, different times and different streets at different times but the codes are codified and can't change. Or won't change. Gotta keep up to the past.

*

Why besides the alliteration is Thursday for the throwback? There's room every day to reminisce. Drama is in the wings waiting to take centerstage of the memory. Be the odor lingering in the mind's nose that goes ignored for sake of eyes, for sake of ears, for sake of skin, for sake of worrying over tomorrow when yesterday ain't even over. Yesterday never had a proper break up. Doesn't it deserve one? Just say it was **mutual.** Nobody will ever know it wasn't.

*

"In Paradise, / Multitudes of letters are sent by crane. / ... No tree lacks a perched phoenix." (Li Shangyin - Emerald Walls)

*

Underworlds and overworlds have varying traditions. Can't plan for everything. The myths leave out too many details. Diaries do the same. Dialogue even more so.

*

The mirror returns the same nigga all the time. The shadow is a shortening and lengthening of the same. It's queer to sense it any other way. Sentiment says that's what exists. Memory can't reconcile with feelings that might suggest there's anything askew in the picture as it is framed.

*

Don't get dead. Not yet. Don't make it a habit. Break as the waves break. Bring the ship to port. Bring the herd upstream along the banks of the river. The ghosts broke and were never repaired. Repairs ain't reparations so who cares about that sort of thing? Should be getting something in return for surviving. Something before the end of the day. Before it gets to the darkest moment.

*

Can't hide the pain. Too much slips out. The face is a traitor. The oblivion knows what refuses to fall between the cracks of life.

Fatigue and disdain catch up to the eyes. In this case, believe the eyes. But this is a case by case situation. Eyes are still suspect. Yet eyes, mouth, nose, all work against keeping it in. Trying to be OK. Mostly to not be bothered by people checking in.

*

Some nights there's nobody to look at. Literally, nothing to see. Not much anyway. Sent to the gulag of the building. Confined to one's own company. Some nights it's welcomed. Other times, it's possible that somebody is looking to break someone. Should quit. Won't though. Not in the mood to go on the market again. Searching takes so much time away from no time to spare. Is there more money to get? Don't want it. The lifestyle that's being lived is built around this check. Did the math. Still doing it. Numbers always on the mind. Calculations reside on the nerve endings. There's an equation for everything. Truth tables and proofs.

*

Thinking twice is one way in which desire proves that it is immortal.

*

If demons possess what do angels do? Is the role of the guardian to prevent this? Which job is easier? Angels can fall but can demons rise?

*

Could get lucky. Found a few bucks a few shifts ago. Found a baggie. Found some free time hiding out in a stall. Why can't the clock be broken in this favor? Time does no favors. Space ain't exactly generous either. But time is money. Space ain't shit. That's why the ghetto is full of niggas who ain't shit either. Was one too. Am one now. Might die not being shit too. But know the value of a minute. Watched too many folks taken before getting a chance to do better, be better. Just simply to be. Don't need to be better. Let a nigga exist. All that or ain't shit, it don't matter. The good die young. The old can't live forever.

*

"crowd in rotation...Somebody can't relate (hol' up) / Stay down with no fakin' (go up) / Top-down..." (Schoolboy Q, 2 Chainz, Saudi)

*

Surrounded. This is America. Could be anywhere. No windows just doors. Walls and shelves. Too level. Too straight. What's the aesthetic? What's being said in this layout? What kind of tax cut did the company get that's not getting passed down to the individuals?

*

"façade is just a fake / Shock horror no escape / Sensationalism for the feed" (X-Ray Spex)

*

Artificial. Right down to the goals. Can't remember childhood fantasies. Had to fake new dreams. Something to fill the confines of the identity. Something to motivate when the energy deteriorates. **Desire** rusts even if it keeps on running. Attraction hangs around the house but doesn't really want to go out anymore. Maybe this puts love out of reach. Romance is a pot not forgotten about but not stirred either.

Discomfort against skin. Discomfort in skin.

*

Get it over with. Get to the part when it's ok to go home to nobody. Make somebody up for some discussion. Clear out the mind. Get some stuff off the chest.

*

So clock finicky and so clock particular. Nothing abstract about how to read the clock. Linear upon a circular face not the depths but sinking. Falling into a shyness. Suffocated by a sentimental timidity. Withdrawn into fears. Scared of what is gone. Too afraid to pursue what might appear next. The old ticker, the heart is wound up and wound too tight and thus skips too many beats. Always aflutter. Imagination is enough bring one to palpations. Too old to be so silly. Too many twilights have brought no tenderness. Give up. The clock, the mirror, the tasks all say it's over. It's too late. This season of life suggests self-love is the only love left. The pirate has become seasick. The sea, dearest ally, turned an enemy.

*

Nature will not stopped. The pigeons make nests in the backroom. Pick at birdfeed and avoid the traps, nets, and catchers.

*

Didn't ask to be a saint nor a martyr. Can't intuit how to exist as an angel. Don't want to be an android. Is this robotic? The intelligence feels artificial. An automaton. The golem. Animated. But not really alive. Even a shrug of a shoulder should be met by approval. Who is the programmer?

*

Is sharing feelings generosity or vanity?

*

Oh, today is just one of those days. A diary is not a memoir. Truth doesn't live in the mood. The moment is only loyal to the emotion.

*

"Nothing thicker than a knife's blade separates happiness from melancholy." (Virginia Woolf - Orlando)

*

Somebody who used to be here is gone. Moved on. The loss is sensed in a lack of a certain something to sense forward to. Not simply look forward to but to feel forward to also. A conversation removed. A similarity severed. Nobody remaining can take up the vacancy. The overall understanding now is much less. To speak is less desirable. To say what's good is polite and to be honest, automatic, but to dig deeper is sadly unwanted. To remain after only reminds of another before. This is no longer the same place although the space is maintained.

*

Extol. Memory is no cave and not a pool. Such Englishisms by such Anglos make mistakes of a basic functioning. Is foxfire closer? Well, at least the sense of decay is put forefront. Memory does indeed bring luminescence to a decaying.

*

Flammerole. Feu follet. OK, to give air back to the English, will o' the wisp: a strange light that attracts travellers from pathways into dangerous marshes or graveyards. (idiomatic) A delusionary **or otherwise unachievable** goal that one feels compelled to pursue.

*

The daydream defeats memory. Memory is a victim and deserves to be. But the daydream only. Not dreams. Niggas ain't got no Rip Van Winkles. No time for sleep.

Daydreams are haphazard. Hazardous for the happening. Might be descended from memory but are not copycats. Take caution. Use it.

*

Native shores? What native shores to return to which from which one was not native. Not native in terms of generations at least. Removed from one place and dropped elsewhere and now this is home? This is the native shore to leave and come back to? No native shores. Pirate dreams arise to declare an attack against such ideas.

*

B=2, L=3, A=1, C=3, K=2 =11=2

N=5, I=9, G=7, G=7, A=1=29=11=2

Just a quick look at a time when one shouldn't be looking: Those with Life Path Number 2 are more likely to seek harmony and peace, and are symbolized by relationships, co-operation, and being considerate and thoughtful of others. People with a Life Path 2 are natural peacemakers...

11 = master number ... more spiritually aware, a visionary, inspiring, charismatic, inventive, a dreamer, idealistic, and a deep thinker....

The challenge for Elevens is to not be overwhelmed by these gifts. Fears and phobias would be the downside of this number .... at times indecisive, impractical, nervous, and moody.

(seventhlifepath.com)

*

Words are spells and yet one takes but a cursory look at these combinations while stealing moments in places that give no space to reading. Less even to writing.

*

Thoughts take shape. Assume a shape. Take long in coming, longer in forming, really forming. Becoming a shape, perhaps, but arriving as a shape is not always admirable. At is OK. It is an eventuality, an event, but as is established and all things established must be destroyed or decay. Build up or breakdown? Those are the only possible destinies / destinations for a thought.

*

The clock's face is symmetrical enough but where are the high cheekbones that are so favorable these days?

*

A bit touched. Touched in the head. Touched by the spirit. A light touch. A soft touch. An easy touch. A touch of the sun. The magic touch. Touch of a button. To be in touch. To be out of touch. Keep in touch. The finishing touch. Get in touch. The golden touch. A touch of class. The Midas touch. Wouldn't touch via a ten-foot pole. To lose touch (see: reality/sanity). Not touch a hair of somebody's head. Not touch a drop. To put somebody in touch. Touchdown. Touchback. Bad touch.

*

The going has always been slow. That has been the problem for too long. Can't get started fast enough then it's all about making up for lost time but that's impossible. Nobody can make up for that.

One can only make it up. One can't even find it no matter how hard one searches.

Lost time is for the travelers moving between life and death, through dimensions, and unseen. Unproven. Whose existence is denied. Whose existence doesn't exist. Not with any substantial proof. Nothing scientific. The age of miracles has passed now it's all about empiricism even though that has also been known to fail.

*

"Love, don't ... falter. / Burning hearts. / Dragged behind. / The horses dancing on the altar. / Hooves breakin' God's. / To diamond dust and stars." (TV on the Radio)

*

It's not fair. The weather is not a fan. It's winter. It is before the spring. The flowers got dead. The sun had to face facts that the day just couldn't go on any longer.

Angels regret the fall. Heaven has vacancies but is filling up fast.

*

Less interesting than one might convince oneself that it is. Once answered, how interesting is the question? Going over and over some hypothetical similarly loses interest in repetition. The angels don't play advocate for the devil. The angels fell once and won't so easily fall again. Not for a weak argument. Not for a played out thought experiment.

And what does it mean to be post-human? What does it mean to speak for non-humans? Nobody can speak on a behalf of a future nor on the behalf for unknowns.

Stop and frisk. 41 shots. Unarmed. Illegal. Detained.

*

Better have no carbon footprint. Better be a vegan. Better ... Nothing ethical under the weight of subjectivity.

*

Pantone 309 will one hour be Pantone 2706.

*

"Story is inhuman..." (Terese Marie Mailhot)

*

Everything here runs the risk of running out. Pay attention. Keep an eye on what is available and what no longer is. Think of the holes that the jeans now own. What was is now something different altogether. Could predict the wearing away. The wearing out. The wear and the tear. But of the hole, fashion statement or garbage pile. Mend, patch, sew up or what?

*

What was radical becomes rudimentary.

*

Imagine the self into situations. Daydream into arms that feel more correct than the ones the real had to offer.

Don't mind spending everyday standing outside in the pouring rain with popsongs coming through, tapping on memory's back door. It doesn't matter anymore. Can't compromise with a compromised conversation among the selves. There will be snow and sleet, wind, humidity, and the seasons won't sleep.

Looked at the window and saw glasses at too harsh an angle. Fell asleep, rolled over, barely salvaged the frame.

Daydreams see something else. Say goodbye to instinct. Even daydreams can't conjure up certain scenes.

Staring at the floor. Get upset and turn to the ceiling. The middle distance is for ignoring.

*

Told too many selves to be patient but now is a different time. Maybe it worked. Maybe calming down has a lot more down to go. Rock bottom has a lot of give. The bottom is broken. The clock works.

*

Been embarrassed by kindness. Who the hell asked anybody to smile?

*

Desires are starting to fall behind. Orbiting isn't about keeping up but keeping a pace. Staying steady. Desires can't even do that right. What else does want want?

Attraction didn't fall asleep. Been up for years on end. See somebody to love every day. No every now and again. No every once in a while. No every once in a lifetime. No not today. No not at all.

*

See dealer for details now through the end times.

*

Parent and child somewhere in the aisles of the evening. Maybe dinner. Maybe a movie. This is not the ocean. Not even an ocean town. Not a tourist town. Not a tourist trap. Maybe it's a Sunday.

Parent and child is out the realm of subjectivity. No parents. Not a child. Don't want to discuss this over dinner nor at therapy.

This is shop talk for a trade that isn't being pursued. Retired. Resigned. Do not rehire.

*

The body needs water but prefers everything else. Is the hangover gone? Is this dehydration? Could get water. Could drink a sports drink. Manual labor is a sport of no sort but works the muscles in similar ways. Sugar-free. Sucralose, aspartame, xylitol. No sugar added. Natural. Nothing artificial.

*

Black Friday and gingivitis. Bleeding gums being bled clean. Next up, back to school sales. Even the grads and dropouts get in on a good deal. Can never have too many pens or underwear.

*

Chewing gum is out of flavor again.

*

Slang is a boomerang. Words come back get reused. Repurposed. Polished and the patina of blackness removed for a more universal usage which means of European descent. The Anglophone beginnings of the word come back to haunt it as it is taken back by English and the descendants of those who first gave and forced English upon the world at hand. The world within range of earshot and the eyesight of phone screen. What was nigga-made will be white-owned soon enough.

No, that's the old school stuff coming out. OK, Xennial. Oregon Trail Generation or closer yet, Generation Sims. Generation Lemmings. Generation Genesis.

The controller doesn't have a button to reset this nor pause it. How about turbo? Beast mode. No, not that. Not there yet, not ready to be a beast. It's not a full moon and this not a bedroom. This isn't the juicy part of the book. But it's another kind of smut.

Get all worked up just thinking about how much further there is to go. Trying to savor that energy. Channel it or flip the switch. Flip the switch. Got stuck on an idea. Stop that. Back to work.

Nigga, please. This is reality. Ain't shit really changed and the floors still ain't clean. Dirty floors and dirty mind. Grew up on dirty jokes, late night TV.

*

Spreading joy? Nah, just mopping up a spill.

*

Little secrets get caught in pants' cuffs. Being short is a dog of non-gender specificity. Being short don't got a dog in a non-sanctioned bout but got a whole lot of problems on the top shelf while keeping the good stuff hidden away down below. Little secrets of dirt trails. Gravel roads. Little secrets of the alley. Little secrets from round back by the dumpsters where the cameras can't witness.

The leaves falling hit tall folks first. Take that.

One kiss don't make a summer and swiping left don't erase a soulmate. What is anybody supposed to do? Everybody has a type – physically, mentally, or emotionally. Can't fit it. Already fit it.

Star-crossed, curly-headed, romance novel ready to be written. Was already wrote by rote. Don't write that. Don't think that. Which is which? What's going on here. The fourth wall jumped the shark long ago.

*

Wild horses don't want to be broken. Ain't no beast asked for that.

Part one. Back to the start out in the fields away from wranglers and rustlers, hats and dungarees. Back to the boring part. The exposition. The horse in the first act will be ridden in the third.

*

So gently, so profoundly, so afraid to be dimmed into the mood of the moment. The trending mood. The two parts of knowing what's going on and also wanting to ignore it.

Don't want to hate on anybody's hustle. That's the rules of the game. So die and let die. It is what it was. At the end of the before. Darkest before the end. How long before? Enough time to unravel the yarn being spun and ready to be cut. But the blade is broken so the yarn continues.

*

The sea stopped searching for sunken treasure. The inventory will never be acknowledged by waves that land on shores. Not attacking just going about its business. The task at metaphorical hand.

Is this a voice for a non-human subject? Were fables? Is artificial intelligence its own voice for its own non-humanness?

*

The stars above the store can't see the coffee cups with coffee not reaching the brims. Spills need to be cleaned so room is left to avoid accidents. Luckily this isn't an allegory so the glass being full doesn't mean anything but has a purpose. The cup is a proposition. The cup is performative. The stars give no gifts of speech acts but a moment can be **taken to** see what the stars said.

Horoscopes are lies but astrology is real. Real enough to believe in, at least, when it is agreeable or when there's a desire to argue. Or, go over the inner catalogue of vagaries and problems that need to be explored no matter how fragile or transparent. Being see-through isn't the same as being seen. That sentence was unnecessary. It was wishful thinking to think anything here was so deep. Pardon the appearance of profundity.

*

Everybody must make a beginning and eventually everybody will get dead. This is the product. This something sold and guaranteed to be bought. Who owns the means of this production?

From each hood according to a hood's ability, to each according to a hood's needs.

And so every nigga knows there are lots of ways to get dead but beginnings are made anyway. Fucking and birthing. Happy born day little nigga.

Nigga is as nigga does. Live by the nigga, die by the nigga.

There are no great sympathies and no primroses. Hip-hop isn't nearly purple enough for that sort of prose and the graffiti lacks a lavendar language.

*

Generosity is the essence of the long con. Cynicism too.

Can never be too trusting. Backs need **to be** watched especially when being patted.

Things turn around quickly. One day, associate of the month, next day it's in the office for some bullshit. Preferences, **privileges**, and vendettas come to the surface. A manager is a devoted friend.

Always ready to do a favor. So much depends upon that wheelbarrow.

Oh, the story and the poem have been confused. It's a confusing time. It's holiday season. It's overdrive but no overtime. Pockets can't get too full or nobody will come back afterwards. There will be no after. But there has to be a morning after and now a song has gotten involved too.

Be careful, don't let all that weigh on the mind. Wouldn't want to make a misstep. Fall off the ladder. Safety first but keep moving. There are times to be exceeding. Meeting is never good enough.

*

The night is the color of mulled wine.

No it's not and this is not the end of the story either.

The story needs a moral.

*

Take the time to see for the first time, a discovery of meeting the wet season, the dry season, night and the day as new as necessary breaking up the monotony of the weather unchanged inside the building kept the same temperature all year round. But instairs is always colder than outstairs. The proximity to core does nothing to keep heat on the ground level lined with freezers, coolers, loading dock. The center is open, allowing whatever warmth was meant for the first floor to graduate to the second level.

Are these details? This is the devil.

The wetness of the rain can be heard in the edges where trucks arrive. The dryness is silent. The wet season is an extension of the real wet season of roots. Creole and Caribbean as well as mainland South. Hurricanes move up the coast. Summer and autumn shift attitudes. Hot and humid turn to thunderstorms. Falling leaves float on flooding in the valleys. Dry season elsewhere is winter here. The wetness freezes, becomes dry. Salt breaks it. The ice has been broken. Now it's wet too. Can be heard under boots. The wet season refuses to give up the game. Water is about that life. Water from roots might rain up here uprooted or water from even further back roots might rain here or rain from undiscovered times might rain here upon parts unknown tucked into the mountains along the river midway up the mainland. The lococentric name for the biggest part of the country. The other pieces are broken off, placed on maps in the odd spots left blue. Sea is vacant enough for the movement of islands packed in too tightly and for even larger landmasses to be removed from the north and moved to the tropics.

What is the psychology of this form? How does this affect a sensing of socioterritorial belonging? The multifold nature of the present and the multiplicity of lineages are left to question how time revises place. The world has been retconned.

*

Wanted to leave early. Want to leave early. Will arrive late. Will be late. The clock is now on the phone. Now, it's not on the wrist anymore. Beginning to forget the back of hand. But it returns for typing. The back of the hand is never too far away for too long. One can be rather textative when one would rather be talkative but there's nobody to talk to sometimes and time drags. Time drags the lake. Dredges up daydreams. Makes light of language as one tries to translate thought. Attempts to convey in a way excommunicated from talking but is often still phonocentric. Can hear a text. Can't really talk an emoji. Icons and logocentric language can be said to varying effectiveness. Shrugging. Upside down smiley face. Is effectivity a word?

*

Word. Word up. Ain't nothing but a word. Wordsmith. Word to ... Don't go there. How many times does it need to be said? Two dead parents.

Word. Word. Ain't a thing. It's all good.

Said self to self. Said self to social. Said social to self. Said social to social. Of course, this will be taken personally and also publicly.

Step aside. Pay attention. Put the phone down. Not supposed to be using the phone any damn way on company time. What if it's an emergency? This is not an emergency. But it has a sense of urgency not easily given to the tasks that require hands.

The clock is all hands on deck as the pirate life comes back to mind. Driftwood daydreams land on shores of concentration. Marooned focus is fucked again.

*

There's a ghost in apparel. This place is haunted. There's a opossum in lawn and garden. There are pigeons in the overstock bins on the top shelf. There's a robot cleaning the aisles. Programmed to scrub. Needs recharging. Takes breaks too. The ghost and the machine never interact. The animals don't pay people much mind. After a while people don't pay the animals much mind either. The ghost is only allegedly around. Can't prove nor disprove the existence of such spirits. But blame goes to the vents. Can air cry as it is recycled? This was all sacred land. Land is sacred. Business is secular. Religion is becoming secular too.

The animals and the machines are not friends but the animals know how to make a meal of wires and a home of the obsolete.

Machines have sensors. The robot can sense obstacles while cleaning the floors. Sometimes the people don't see what's in the way. The machine is on the phone if something gets in its way.

Sends a text. That is an emergency. The machines don't take anything personally. The animals are not social creatures. The air vents let it all out on random strangers passing underneath. The ghost won't shed a tear as long as ... Oh, stand by ... Stand ... By ... And finds a way to embrace the music piped into the place. Gets tired of the in-store radio but sings along anyway. Maybe. The singing can neither be proved nor disproved. Echoes are tricky that way.

*

What's next to come from Mars? What news is new from the rover? Is anybody going back to the moon anytime soon? Space has so much more to be explored and so much more to be ruined by human footprints.

Is there life out there? How does it work? Is there a world of asexuals? A place where alone is more than good enough but is complete? Nobody is suggesting singularity as missing something. Some conversations are better off as monologues but not in mixed company.

No sense in saying some stuff to some folks. Don't deserve the information nor the entertainment. Can't relate or want to relate a bit too much. Such conversations are of little consequence and simply prompt discussions that would be better off unspoken. Why does everybody need to know about everybody else's lives? Some things can remain in house.

*

"a small mistake of nature" (George Eliot - the Mill on the Floss)

*

Honey buns are one dollar or lesser grade ones are two for one dollar. There is rice for $1.88. Takes 90 seconds to cook. There are chips for 82¢. Don't bring lunch to work anymore. No desire to eat too well there. Could be cheaper but what a bad time to try to enjoy oneself. And health can be thrown to the wind once one gets around to being too miserable to even be mad.

*

Even autobiography is only semi-autobiographical.

*

By Jove. Dear God. ¡Ojala! The truth is slower than molasses and only half as sweet. So why the exclamations?

Prologue: there is a cold front coming in. That means something that's why it was said. Before the weather changed a whole lot of air had to move in. Then there would be a mess of things. Plans might need to be put off. An excuse. A reason to play parent to a change of plans. A real reason. The truth.

But this was before. The after will be up to no good soon.

*

Lost count of blessings as abundance often gets misplaced while multitudes take effort to manage. The good is gone. Hidden. What remains to be seen is what the curses will blossom into.

*

Bittersweet treacle flows overseas. And that means nothing right now. Nothing twee is gonna help.

A friend died. Found out here. Stuck in here. There's no space to process what comes next other than the quiet. Don't want this silence. Not yet.

Consider this an introduction to the after.

*

Perpetual anhedonic but professional enabler. If fun can be had, go get it. It's not for this but for those and that, enjoy.

*

Pillow talk and bedroom eyes. Small talk and white lies. Red, gold, and green. Red, gold, and green. Love is an addiction. The withdrawal is worse. It's been a decade of detoxing. Self-medicating and diagnosing.

*

Worthlessness. Devalued.

*

Wallowing in these thoughts won't work. Been trying to live the hard life. Have no desire to avoid difficulty. It is deserved.

*

Tend to be of sparse tears although tears should be freer. Yet, unhappiness hasn't a need to be seen nor heard. Prefer the bed in moments such as these. Whisper to the self to do as one pleases although pleasure is unwanted and altogether unpleasant. Hate favorite shows and don't desire the best of foods. Top shelf or well, it's all the same drunkenness. That's OK. That's alright. That is better than bad but not good. Well enough.

*

Always at the ready to use melancholy as a good-natured weapon on behalf of the world at hand. Or a tool. A tool. Do no harm. Keep it clean. Fix it don't break it. Too much is already broken. Was broken before. Was broken as day broke. And breaks as wave break. As cane rises up, break, and rum dreams roll in.

*

Don't dream much. Don't want to know what the few dreams worth remembering mean either. Interpretations never go the right way. When the dreams go awry it's worse than when the stars do. Worse still than how the cards can tell truths nobody asked for. Worse than the alphabet carved into wood. Prediction and prophecy are one thing but voices from within those are something to worry about. Nothing is worthless to some deeper aspect of the self.

*

Are tragedies the product of passion?

*

Always one more reason to be sorry.

Under blue moon. Stargazing. Forgot how a kiss feels. Won't do no good remembering now. Already behind the eight ball. Tasks are going slower than usual and there's a reason but not a good one as to why.

Some say clumsy but the world just isn't built right. Things fall over. Things need to be picked up again. People too. Takes up a lot of time.

What do the stars know about stagnation?

This was supposed to be better. This was supposed to be for a few months. This was supposed to be before the seasons changed.

*

Too much has been complicated over time. Time the great divider. The common denominator. When does one belong? When does one belong together. Can't close eyes and try to dream. All there is is to notice. To let in the light and darkness and the words of the songs not chosen but heard and approved of. Words of childhood. Words that still stand to this day.

*

Someday ain't today. Not a star yet. Not big time. Nobody to care about. Nothing of value given to the bigger picture. Another ain't-shit nigga that won't supposed to be shit no goddamn way.

Then again, always did go about shit the wrong damn way. Practicality is a piss poor lay. If it's time to fuck or be fucked might as well get past pragmatism and work on having some fun. Or giving some fun. Can't get no fun. Can't accept it. Can't understand it. Ain't had fun since childhood done went colder than this coffee being sipped bit by bit to get to the end of the shift, end of this phase.

It's all phases. Work is a bad habit but will be dropped eventually. In death or retirement. But everything ends.

*

Ghosts ain't got nowhere to go. Rather stuck here. Stay damn nearby and close. Call misery a creature comfort and a place to call home.

*

Will be all moved into a wound by the morning. A two-story scar on the edge of town.

*

Too tired of this to keep on hanging in there. Ain't much left to say about too much of anything else. The grind won't get off this back. Turning to dust. Back to dust but ain't got dead yet for no good reason.

*

Body parts and attitudes sprawled through the thoughts.

*

The body refuses to cooperate. What the self wants the corpse will not give. How many hours at rest does it need? Waking only for work and never for its own good. The collective good of the self.

*

There's no reason to be awake nor alive. But somebody somewhere loves someone and that is supposed to make it all worthwhile or better or something.

*

Didn't want to get out of bed again. Stayed in there until the last possible minute before work. Should've stayed there, taken the punishment for it later and just refused to contribute to the system.

It's the holidays and celebrating is not a thing when work wants all hands on deck to sell this shit.

Then it's not the holidays but there's another reason why no days off will be approved. There's always a way for a job to ruin a life.

DAWN

"any cast line of shadow

would indicate a curve; the distance between

one and not,   an arc of circumference." (Ed Roberson)

*

"... the words The End never arrive at best moment, fairy tales have ample time to deteriorate, in life." (Luisa Valenzuela - Dark Desires and the Others)

*

One: a new day has arrived.

Other: it was necessary.

One: it was.

*

Other: a door is being unloaded now from a lumber store truck.

One: well, what a wonderful way to enter a day.

Other: it's one way.

One: remember that Goines' line about not being able to afford a doorknob on a backdoor?

Other: oh sure every time somebody come asking for money.

One: ain't got nothing to give anyway.

Other: not even no advice.

*

"Another promise fallen through / Another season passes by ... never took the smile away from anybody's face / And that's a desperate way to look / For someone who is still a child" (Big Country)

*

One: still feel or at least still wanna feel young.

Other: today's days are over. Today is different. Deal with it.

One: OK. Look at it this way. Up bright and early. That's something. That's a change.

Other: the lawyers are up too. Walking down the avenue. Can't wait to get to arguing.

One: who can?

Other: is there really any other way to really get going?

One: gotta get those emotions going.

Other: even love is an argument.

One: no, it's not.

Other: stop. Lol. It's too early for this.

One: just wait till later. Then it's really on.

Other: can't wait.

One: don't have to. Later is only a matter perspectives.

Other: no disagreement here.

One: that was too easy.

Other: or was it?

*

"Love and build, love and work, love and fight. Always love first. Anything placed before love will fail." (Sister Souljah - Midnight and the Meaning of Love)

*

Other: went out for breakfast. Wanted a treat. Got one for sure.

One: really?

Other: well, there was this mouse.

One: nobody knows how to act around rodents.

Other: take a picture. Post it and then tell the manager.

One: or let it go.

Other: never.

One: make a spectacle.

Other: but not necessarily a complaint. Can't keep all the vermin under control in a big city.

One: but hold high priced places to higher standards?

Other: maybe.

One: seems certain places get more flack than other places though.

Other: true. Unfair enough.

One: so, how was the food?

Other: don't know. Settled for a cup of coffee and some light entertainment instead. Breakfast theater.

*

"The exercise, a delicate and secret asceticism to guess the enigmatic desire of the other, utterly enchanted the body." (Anne Garréta - Not One Day)

*

One: how does a werewolf just go to back to work on Monday after a full moon?

Other: easy. Life just be that way. Have to keep up appearances. Maintain a routine. A lifestyle.

One: that's the reality.

Other: for almost everybody.

One: just be careful before somebody decides to bite the hand that feeds.

*

"Nothing moves in the dark but danger." (Chester Himes - Cotton Comes to Harlem)

*

Other: don't come in here with bad news nor a bad attitude.

One: it's just a way of showing affection.

Other: how so?

One: it's honest. Fearless.

Other: still don't enjoy it.

One: didn't enjoy last night either but dealt with it.

Other: OK, do tell.

One: not much to talk about. Forget it.

*

One: what's next?

Other: after breakfast?

One: after life?

Other: heaven is trap house. Who'd want to go there?

One: so, zombies then?

Other: that or ghosts.

One: then, zombie sounds better. Thoughtless but tactile.

Other: ghosts must be so lonely.

One: and both are feared.

Other: who has it worse djinn or fairies?

One: definitely djinn. The lamp is a pretty shitty place to live.

Other: do fairies have it good?

One: maybe wings are a good consolation prize for such long lives of quiet sorrow. Magic's gotta get boring after awhile.

Other: magic is so mundane.

One: and so many needy folks asking for paranormal favors has to get old too.

Other: that's why the smart angels stayed in heaven.

One: and the bad ones have grown tired of playing games.

Other: Lucifer is on vacation.

One: a holiday to rival Christmas.

*

" ... if there is a delay it can only mean ... a trap ... hide this diary, invent some explanation and wait..." (Adolfo Bioy Casares - The Invention of Morel)

*

Other: the golem.

One: the original robot.

Other: these mechanical servants were never to be trusted. Certainly, something would go wrong.

One: go off the rails.

Other: at least the train has rails, tracks, stations, terminals.

One: what does the golem have other than commands?

Other: one cannot imagine the golem happy.

*

One: not ready for bed yet.

Other: why? Thought the night was rough. Thought it was long. Can't take much more.

One: yeah, makes more sense to spend some time on the self rather than recharge for somebody else.

*

Other: Nothing is what it was when it first started. Endings occur where endings occur. Don't want to decide when but it'll be over when it's over and there will be no changing that. Nothing to be done then. Love isn't ever enough. Or love is everything and it's not around here anymore. Could work with semantics a bit more. Don't want somebody else's bad feelings on this conscious. It's nobody's fault. Or it's everybody's. Nobody is innocent. Maybe there wasn't anything happening here in the first place. Now, this could be the last place. That's where everything is found, isn't it?

*

One: Red, gold, and green. Dreams keep getting older all the time. Not a superhero now, not a villain either. The comic book life ain't ever gonna happen. This ain't a eulogy but it's a goodbye.

*

"...busted fairies... the word heaven... assemble in limbo..." (Stephen Jonas - Postlude)

*

"filled to the beautiful brim with love" (Ted Joans)

*

Other: so much more to give.

One: so much more to receive.

*

Stable chance thesis: that in any given possible world, any pair of intrinsic duplicate physical setups with the same chances of being subject to the same external influences must yield the same chances.

*

One: objective chance made this happen.

Other: made or correlated?

One: maybe it doesn't matter.

Other: maybe. Maybe is all one ever has to depend on. Maybe is the constant and the variable.

*

Other: wanted to see something coming. The view was obscured. The vision was compromised by the viewer. Didn't want to worry about the potential. Whether positive or negative, predictions are filled with anxiety. Looking forward is a risky proposition. Ahead is around a bend, out of sight but always on the mind. Tomorrow might not be first love but is a rebound that nobody can shake. Always getting back together even though nobody is really happy in the arrangement.

*

One: couldn't make sense of what there was to sense. **This is** a romance and as such is also a mystery. Questionable evidence, clues, hunches, and jumping to conclusions are the stuff love is made of. Or what will be termed love in the official reports filed by the crooked cops.

*

Other: together. A few memories to share and some more to make.

One: hopefully. Something to look forward to.

Other: forward to or forward toward?

One: forward into.

Other: access granted.

One: the code has been broken.

Other: the magic word to break the seal.

*

One: lost again.

Other: can't be found or don't want to be?

One: a lot of both. A new day is never all that it's cracked up to be. The darkest has passed but the brightness isn't much better.

Other: the thoughts that accompany the after are too late for the day in which / on which / upon which those thoughts were formed.

One: yes, afterthoughts but not always regrets.

Other: not always anything. Hyperbole is hindsight's selectivity speaking.

One: but...

Other: but nothing.

*

Other: what will the end be?

One: might be too soon to know.

Other: venture a guess.

One: guesses get people in trouble. Certainty is preferred.

Other: preferred but certainly no fun at all.

One: what has fun ever done for anybody?

Other: it made this possible, didn't it?

One: there's no correct answer to that question.

Other: but it was asked.

One: and it's no fun at all.

Other: but it's playful.

One: it's work.

Other: is everything work?

One: it is. It's a robot's world now. Tasks and more tasks.

Other: can one be tasked to have fun?

One: one cannot have fun. It is unable to be owned.

Other: does not compute.

One: refuses to be computed.

Other: this intelligence is so artificial.

One: synthetic.

*

"Off to the next episode, money to get

Can't be slippin' and snoozin' and cattin' off" (E-40)

*

One: day has broken.

Other: again?

One: again and again. The day is broken.

Other: into hours, minutes, seconds.

One: into hard feelings and bad ideas.

*

"There's no time here, not any more ... This is the trap. This is nowhere, and it's forever." (Mark Fisher - in reference to Sapphire and Steel)

*

Other: can't keep up. Don't really want to. It's ok to be outdated.

One: relax into ignorance.

Other: naïveté.

One: can't watch every show. Read every book. Listen to every song.

Other: the joy is in the choosing. The freedom from the syllabus and the rigidity of schedules.

One: still got to work around work though.

Other: but nobody is assigning what's supposed to be important anymore.

One: wonder if anything important was ever really assigned.

Other: the important part of the assignment was trying to figure out what was important. Now it is to figure out **what** is important.

One: the is requires keeping up.

Other: but only in ways that work for one at that moment. Or for future moments. Being outdated doesn't mean not planning for the future. It just means not paying attention to everything.

One: filtering.

Other: and erasing if it needs to come to that.

*

"The sun coming up in the morning is enough." (Ralph Ellison - Shadow and Act)

*

One: landscape doesn't always agree with the sensibilities. Took trains and rode busses across the country. Nothing really fit the mood but the ambience of a place will adjust an attitude. Some places is for lonely folks. Some ain't. Hard to tell which is which. Some parties ain't for everybody. Some bars got that conversation running from end to end. Some cafés are all chatter. Kindness comes in odd dosages. Strangers ain't so bad when one gets sad enough to settle for anybody.

*

"hand-in-hand walking down ... streets of gold

Six feet below ... a better place ... in a better place ... gonna make ... a better place ... Every night (every night) And every day ... fade away" (Kane Brown)

*

Other: got time to think. Being away is good for that. Even if it's somebody else being away. Fuck, was it really space to think?

*

"Even love, that exquisite torturing emotion, left its subtle traces on the countenance." (Nella Larsen - Passing)

*

One: what broke the angel's fall?

Other: which angel?

One: any one who took the leap.

Other: so Lucifer?

One: so Lucifer.

Other: well, one must imagine Eden as overgrown so perhaps the highest branches in the canopy of orchard. The crescent was fertile way back then. Lucifer fell into an abundance of leaves. If one is to be literal.

One: and if not?

Other: and if not, then nothing broke the fall. The fall itself was merely the falling out of love with God.

*

"It's funny what a little time does" (Mickey Guyton)

*

Other: how does anybody know when to leave?

One: nobody knows. Not even in all those suicide notes.

Other: but people leave.

One: some people have no other choice.

Other: or it feels that way. It's the only feeling left. The only feeling that won't leave.

*

"got the horses in the back

Horse tack is attached

Hat is matte black

Got the boots that's black to match

Ridin' on a horse" (Lil Nas X)

*

One: those old movies were sure telling some stories.

Other: straight lying.

One: straight up.

Other: and straight is the right word too.

One: word.

Other: for real.

*

Other: ever think about how the country folk live? How It might be in those places? Can't imagine a small town nonetheless fields to till.

One: nah. There's a reason folks went to the big cities.

Other: being a farmhand can't be too bad.

One: ain't no job any good.

Other: gotta do something. Ain't nothing free.

One: staying Black is enough work, ain't it?

Other: yeah, but it don't make no money.

One: not for Black folks.

*

One: wasn't born for this.

Other: nobody was born for nothing.

*

"[the] hand thunders indifference" (Joyce Mansour)

*

Other: hard to get comfortable sometimes.

One: sending hugs from here to there.

Other: best wishes too.

One: yes, stay strong.

*

Other: an embrace **isn't** always wanted. Skin on skin isn't for everybody nor for every situation. Maybe it's a question of taste. Maybe it's conditioning. Maybe it's just the skin itself. Hard to tell. Don't care. Just don't touch. But find a different way to show love. That much is wanted.

*

One: when white folks catch a cold black folks catch pneumonia.

Other: everybody sick but some are sicker than others.

One: one stays on sick.

Other: trying to keep some folks stuck on sick.

One: some things never change.

Other: is anybody looking for the antidote?

One: yes, those who are affected the most.

Other: so, same old same old.

One: same new too.

*

Other: is this love?

One: it's a conversation.

Other: is it romance?

One: certainly.

*

"lived in circumstance ... Lived a fairy tale ... Made a promise the truth will never fail" (the Veldt)

*

One: can one read one's way right out of hell?

Other: maybe if somebody wants to bore Cerberus to death.

*

Other: meanwhile back at the ranch.

One: it was a dark and stormy night.

Other: once upon a time.

One: there was a fugituve on the lam.

Other: a case of mistaken identity.

One: amnesia and missing time.

Other: alien abduction.

One: nobody buys that alibi.

Other: well, too late. Ridin' the rails now. Be out west before too long.

One: fascists sure do keep the trains running on time.

Other: even after the end of the world.

One: just gotta get back to grab the kid.

Other: then it's off to the center of the hollow earth.

One: ain't no mobster angels and preacher zombies in there.

Other: just robots, the fey, and leviathan.

One: safe enough to really start a family.

Other: and live happily ever after.

*

One: the grind never stops.

Other: facts. But imagine if it did.

One: then there'd be more time to be in love.

*

Other: overslept but didn't overdream.

*

One: would love to stay awake forever but the body betrays desires.

*

Other: don't really have a favorite song anymore. Not even a band to find too soothing.

One: why?

Other: nothing feels good in the ears anymore. Maybe music, in general, never did. Feels a good waste of sounds sometimes.

One: some folks claim to get goosebumps from hearing certain things. Some songs get in the skin. Or the nerves beneath maybe.

Other: well, from experience, neither senses bother to care about any of it.

One: maybe it's more a question of instincts than of taste. Maybe some folks weren't born to enjoy certain things.

Other: tried to train the ears. Wasted too much time on the effort.

*

"crazy dada nigga ... given to fantasy ... far out esoteric bullshit"
(Ishmael Reed - Yellow Back Broke-Down Radio)

*

Other: can see a new horizon

One: under the blazing sky?

Other: can hear the music playing.

One: can see the banners fly.

Other: can say this is the world that the movies always said there would be.

One: this ain't the hood. This **is the** imagination of John Hughes come to life.

Other: life imitates some stuff that might be considered art.

*

One: is this love?

Other: would sooner call it a cypher.

One: well, better than a battle.

Other: sure beats the mainstream.

"... believe god is immortal, irrational, / and sometimes tired. The sun, it seems, worships only the bodies of the young ... Only petty gods want to be worshipped." (Zeina Hashem Beck)

*

Other: saints and sinners.

One: nothing in between.

Other: nothing else.

One: one performs miracles and the other misery.

Other: one to praise and one to relate to.

One: one for candles.

Other: one for the shadows.

*

One: it's a new day.

Other: again?

One: it was necessary.

*

Other: sometimes it's easier to show sympathy for the clouds rather than for the rain.

One: for love, the clouds let go of the rain.

Other: for meteorological conditions also and more so.

One: but what about the desire to personify?

Other: what about it?

One: is it natural or just another tradition passed down without too much argument?

Other: it's incorrect and nothing more.

One: it's artistic.

Other: there are no artists here.

One: it's poetic.

Other: then try being prosaic for a change.

One: or maybe just rhetorical.

*

"Dancing on the astral plane / On holy water cleansing rain / Floating through the stratosphere ... Is there a way ... to shine without fear" (Valerie June)

*

One: at the end of the day.

Other: it's all cliché.

*

Other: it's always darkest.

One: where there ain't no light.

*

One: six in one hand.

Other: two in the bush.

One: half dozen in the other.

Other: in the other who?

One: knock knock.

Other: knock knock who?

One: knock before entering.

Other: entering what, where, or whom?

One: same difference.

Other: slippery slope.

One: when wet.

Other: be careful. Exercise caution.

One: for at least 20 **minutes a** day to maintain a healthy heart.

*

"Ain't shit sweet ... got two lions ... got ten sheep ... Street math ... got three eyes open, one in the back ... Just in case ... niggas get out of character" (Young M.A.)

*

"...each image is shifted

back & forth

between gales & the apparition of gales" (Will Alexander - Inside the Ghost Volcano)

*

Other: candy.

One: something to melt in the mouth.

Other: to go from hard to soft enough to chew.

One: to flavor the saliva. Be worth the work of slurping.

Other: reminder of visiting old folks.

One: thinking about getting there one day too.

Other: be getting there soon if there's no wrench thrown in the works.

One: if **the** machine stays greased.

*

"Kills bugs dead. Redundancy is syntactical overkill" (Harryette Mullen - Kills Bugs Dead.)

*

One: said it once.

Other: will always say it again.

One: yeah yeah.

Other: whereas one "nah" would suffice.

One: but the other way was twice as fun.

Other: half as funny though.

One: not cool at all.

Other: nothing ever is.

*

Other: is this love?

One: it's a schtick.

Other: is it any good?

One: could be worse.

*

One: what to do with all that time away from work? What is time "off" from?

Other: there are always other duties to get to. There's no real free time.

One: sleep is punished. Rest is punished. There is no respite.

Other: something will go undone. The weekend ends nothing.

One: to-do lists grow and side hustles and unpaid work are fretted over.

Other: there's more anxiety on the day off than on the days on.

One: dread both the weekdays and the weekends.

Other: and vacations have more days and more problems.

One: but still gonna sleep in late.

Other: definitely.

One: the day will be over when it's time to get up.

Other: and the world can just deal with that.

*

Other: the Promised Land.

One: the land of milk and honey.

Other: gonna go on getting lost looking for better places.

One: look at the skies and listen to advice from the wind and spirits to be the guides.

Other: ouija boards, tarot, divination of any sort.

One: gotta hold out hope that the dead have something to say to the living so the same mistakes aren't made again.

Other: ancestors make better guardian angels than the angels do.

One: one can hope.

Other: one can ask.

*

One: looking for a new show to watch. Got no time to watch it but ready to get sucked into a couple of episodes.

Other: should just start at the end and read a few think pieces online.

One: is this entertaining?

Other: it's realistic.

One: is it relaxing?

Other: stop asking for so much.

One: OK. What about another beer?

Other: think of the waistline.

One: fuck keto. Tired of gin and seltzer.

Other: have coffee.

One: but it's almost time to go to bed.

Other: that depends. Bedtime is malleable. How much sleep does anybody need?

One: it's more about the dreams.

Other: what if one doesn't remember the dreams?

One: then try harder. Read about lucidity. Keep a dream diary. Tell the self to remember. Make memory never take a break.

Other: that's a lot of work.

One: there is no such a thing as relaxation. There are no breaks.

*

Other: Armageddon might mean mount of assembly.

One: well that's better. What a nice little get together.

Other: can't wait to see who is resurrected for the party.

*

One: if one is wrong, in which direction is one wrong?

Other: well, does one think about thinking as traveling?

One: talking is certainly a trip.

*

Other: could there be fallen angels walking the earth?

One: who'd hang around here when it'd be so easy to leave?

*

One: wonder when first contact will occur. When alien life will meet human life.

Other: maybe nothing is out there.

One: maybe it's nothing people can understand.

Other: maybe aliens understand people enough to not stop by for a visit.

*

Other: been waiting to find out what truth is out there for decades now.

One: what if the truth has been debunked?

Other: debunking doesn't mean deceased. Just look at the systems still in place today.

One: democracy.

Other: as tied to money.

*

One: it's too early to get too deep. Whatever happened to keeping it light?

Other: not really down with no small talk.

One: what if being profound was just a phase?

*

Other: betrayal is not reciprocation but it's a product of feelings. Were those feelings ever mutual is another question. Were the feelings even ever between two people or just in one person and released upon another? Nonetheless, betrayal lies in wait. Is even dormant but wakes and pounces. Sometimes one even betrays oneself when certain feelings aren't mutual.

One: the pirate will never prefer the prairie of the cowpoke and angels and androids have different ways of assessing preferences. No one asked to be built to certain specifications but end up becoming something specific. Something specific to the local conditionings or move to better localities. Movement is another sort of adapting.

*

Other: God's green earth is becoming less green.

One: God's grey earth.

Other: the grey grey concrete of home.

One: young greyhorns out on the cattle drive.

Other: looking a little grey around the gills.

One: the only green is the greenlight to keep on going down this path.

*

"Irrepressible rhythm ... How easily one falls into step ... Chance, for method betrays itself through too much consistency, too much

saturation, and the excess of signification leaves the suspicion of premeditation from which one must protect oneself from if one wants to be believed and exonerated on account of one's naïveté."
(Anne Garréta - Not One Day)

*

One: is this love?

Other: it's an inquiry and this the answer.

*

Other: American Landscape is on the mind.

One: Allan D'Arcangelo's painting?

Other: that would be the one. The highway, the arrows, the red and yellow just popped in.

One: maybe it's a call from the inside to find a sense of direction.

Other: but in a popular way?

One: maybe in a pop art way. The painting isn't exactly popular.

Other: not where it's displayed.

One: even in a museum, it's hard to be popular.

Other: who goes to those places anyway?

One: students and artists.

Other: there's gotta be a bigger fanbase than that.

One: it's more than some folks ever get.

Other: it's a bit of a bonus love that the everyday person may never experience.

One: some people's work will never come to mind.

Other: even work that is seen every day by the thousands.

One: the mall cleaners do work that never comes to mind.

One: the work goes unloved. Hopefully, the workers don't.

*

One: never felt cute.

Other: haven't deleted yet.

*

"Something in[side] has to break (out). There's something in[side] that should be born. Something that needs to be pushed out. Struggle. Give birth to it. A force. There is a force in[side] that wants to explode ... [haven't] let it." (Luisa Valenzuela - Dark Desires and the Others)

*

One: is it a holiday?

Other: it's just a regular day.

One: the city feels less full.

Other: regular folks can take regular days too.

One: sometimes. It's hard to come by in some of these places.

Other: those little places with just enough staff to get through the work.

One: those places that ask a lot and give little.

Other: those places. Are those places for regular people?

One: regular people don't always see it that way especially when regular people are on regular schedules and the other regular people are not.

Other: there are many regulars.

One: that's what the businesses hope for. Regular keep the wheels spinning. Can't live off of the random nor the occasional.

*

Other: is this love?

One: it is a game.

Other: who is winning?

One: it's not that kind of game.

Other: does everybody get a trophy?

One: nobody wants one. One wants something better than that.

*

"The truth hurts, and so does yesterday

What good is love if it burns bright, and explodes in flames" (Janelle Monae)

*

One: dropping bombshells.

Other: spilling that tea.

One: staying up on that dirt.

Other: got the receipts.

One: it ain't gossip if it happened.

Other: but call it a rumor if all the other words sounds too harsh.

*

"lost reality somewhere between the pines" (Tiera)

*

Other: is it time to wake up?

One: could stay asleep longer.

Other: could be awake longer.

One: could start now and end earlier if everything gets done sooner.

Other: could just not do anything.

One: it all needs to get done at some point.

Other: or what?

*

One: hands are tied.

Other: tongue is tied too.

One: can't make a move.

Other: can't make a sound.

One: wouldn't want it any other way.

Other: would never allow it.

*

Other: that one movie.

One: and that one scene.

Other: think it was enjoyable.

One: yes, mutually so.

Other: kind of different.

One: something unsuspecting.

Other: but heartwarming.

One: might have cried.

Other: can't watch it again.

One: that's for sure.

*

"... sort of snaky ... but to follow was the safest route..." (Margaret Verble - Maud's Line)

*

One: serpentine.

Other: such is the way of evasion.

One: narrative switchbacks.

Other: flip-flopping.

One: wishy-washy.

Other: indecisive or deliberate.

One: maybe both.

Other: just stay close behind the words.

One: fill the phrase's rear view.

Other: don't let the debate become a drag race.

One: don't drag it out to Le Mans either.

*

Other: L=A=N=G=U=A=G=E

One: equals crickets

Other: the sound is a pin dropping.

*

"Despair isn't a conduit for love." (Terese Marie Mailhot - Heart Berries)

*

Other: wanted to write something the other day. Don't know what. Didn't even know about what. Maybe just a note. A note can be nice. People enjoy notes. Especially notes beginning in dear and ending as XOXO. But who would the note be addressed to?

One: wanted to read something the other day. Don't know what. Didn't know about what either. Something bigger than a text. Wanted to make reading a form of resilience.

*

One: what's the best way to kill time?

Other: letting it live.

*

Other: bored, hungry, tired.

One: but which one the most?

Other: bored.

One: well, apparently, conversation isn't working for that but it's also not helping with the tired part either. So, at least it's boring but not enough to put anybody to sleep.

Other: can it make a sandwich?

Only: a bullshit sandwich and humble pie for dessert.

*

One: remember when the radio was worth turning on?

Other: not really but there weren't many other choices in the days before the internet once listening to the same old collection got even older.

One: still though, miss the random. Miss not knowing what was next. Enjoyed the DJs too. Not every DJ but the ones with some stories were nice.

Other: never was one for too many stories. Can't stand talk radio or worse yet the late night shows.

One: but a good interview...

Other: no interviews are good. It's all so rehearsed.

One: what about movies? Those are rehearsed.

Other: movies are awful too. Prefer a good bit of silence and a window.

*

"These are the sounds of gears grinding

These are the round levers

These are the sounds behind the machines

These are the voices of modern industry

These are the voices

These are the voices" (Fishbone)

*

Other: so what's the deal?

One: what deal?

Other: the big deal, of course.

One: oh, that deal.

Other: yes, that deal.

One: well, the deal is a distribution of some sort. Usually cards. The big deal, on the other hand might be anything worth a discussion. Anything news and / or noteworthy.

Other: well done.

One: could be better. Could use deal as both a noun and verb but there's really no big deal as a verb, is there?

One: not really.

*

One: once upon a time.

Other: on a small deserted island.

One: there lived a unicorn.

Other: and it was all alone.

One: except for.

Other: one little bat.

One: the unicorn and the bat were friends.

Other: there was no other choice.

One: but the two rarely spoke.

Other: it was hard for the bat to stay up late in the day and it was equally hard for the unicorn to stay up too late into the night.

One: neither knew how to write so no letters were exchanged.

Other: just gifts of berries, fruits, pebbles, and that sort of thing.

One: this was a good friendship.

*

Other: what's good?

One: not much. Still tired. Haven't slept. Didn't eat.

Other: and whose fault is that?

One: whose fixing could it be?

Other: both are one in the same.

One: both are too tired and too hungry to change a thing.

Other: so, it's all good?

One: yeah, not bad.

*

One: is this love?

Other: it is a treasure hunt.

One: who has the map?

Other: who lost the chest?

One: or hid the chest?

*

Other: to after death.

One: to the edge of every day's most quiet innocence.

Other: to upset God's most glorious misgivings.

One: to the tempest.

Other: and trembling chest.

One: and the **heights'** faintness.

Other: may a maelstrom be the swirling of love about the selves.

One: ready to die in the sea.

Other: down among the demons who live in envy.

One: and whose jealousy is a fruit untouched by such sailors as this.

Other: and here.

*

One: oh, winged narrative

Other: come be a morning's dew upon these words.

One: thus may this suffering be relieved here.

Other: and relived there.

One: sleepless.

Other: triggering and steadfast.

One: blooming.

Other: ripening.

One: cooked.

Other: eaten.

One: expelled.

Other: hands washed.

One: ass cleaned.

Other: order out of order.

*

Other: this is the Pomodoro technique.

One: can it be the pomeranian technique instead? Those little dogs are so cute.

Other: anything that will more efficiently use time.

One: dogs can't tell time.

Other: can't say "time" either.

One: has it been 25 minutes yet?

Other: not by a dog's age

One: but a break would still be pretty nice.

Other: it's coming.

One: not soon enough but don't look at the clock.

Other: is this technique supposed to be used for conversations?

One: it's supposed to be used for work, tasks, chores.

Other: so, yes.

One: is it time?

Other: close enough.

*

Other: this could be love.

One: or a bit of undigested beef.

Other: no, this the ghost of love past, present, and future come to give a warning.

One: what warning warrants such heeding?

Other: this one.

One: which one?

Other: this one, this one simple and pure warning.

One: which is?

Other: don't get strung along for too long.

*

One: Nyquil

Other: Dayquil

*

Other: breaking rocks in the hot sun.

One: fought the law and the law won.

*

One: are all romances romantic comedies?

Other: what? Hell no. Too many are tragedies.

One: oh, so Titanic wasn't funny?

Other: not as funny as Gatsy.

One: was Titanic a satire.

Other: it was ironic.

One: no, that's just the way it was watched.

Other: whoa, deja vu. Has this conversation happened before?

One: maybe it was in another book.

Other: so what place meant was not much?

One: yup, the same stuff happens from place to place.

Other: was the other book a comedy?

One: it was a love story.

Other: that doesn't sound right. It wasn't a story.

One: it was a love.

Other: it was a tragedy.

One: it was funny.

Other: oh, the irony.

One: oh, the satire.

Other: how romantic.

One: how comedic.

Other: how familiar.

One: already seen.

Other: haunting.

One: always already.

Other: just read an article about depressed people using hyperbole.

One: never read it. Never read those sorts of things. That stuff is the worst.

Other: sometimes.

One: all the time.

Other: it's happening again. This conversation took place somewhere else.

One: where did it take the place?

Other: here. It brought it here.

One: how romantic. Love will find a way.

Other: oh no, it was tragic. That conversation was trying to escape the tragedy.

One: did it?

Other: won't know till the end.

One: oooo, a twist.

*

Other: why don't all novels employ novel approaches?

One: ask a writer?

Other: why not a reader?

*

One: ever miss having an audience?

Other: not really.

One: pretty sure somebody is always watching.

Other: what about while sleeping?

One: especially then.

Other: creepy.

One: it's a creepy world. Full of spirits and myths.

Other: truths and metaphors.

*

"Always been about time more than been about pay" (Jidenna)

*I

Other: the day off is getting away.

One: go get it. Take this horse.

Other: don't know how to ride.

One: a country nigga who can't ride a horse?

Other: a contemporary nigga from the city who can't drive either.

One: maybe the day deserved to get away.

Other: didn't want it anyway. It was a mutual breakdown.

*

One: the fairy tale and the folk tale have different sets of morals.

Other: one is at the hand of the supernatural and the other is at the whims of a good strong back and a sharp wit.

One: as long as there's no moral, it's ok.

Other: a moral is a dangerous thing.

*

"What is out of nature never thrives." (George Eliot - The Mill on the Floss)

"Caught up in circles / confusion is nothing new." (Cindi Lauper)

*

Other: no help is ever really helpful.

One: what help was needed?

Other: none.

*

One: kind of cloudy.

Other: can't quite remember?

One: no getting ready for rain?

*

Other: would love to just go for a ride.

One: don't really want to drive.

Other: hop a train, take a bus.

One: and go where?

Other: somewhere far from here but not so far as to not be able to come back.

One: a daytrip?

Other: yeah, that's all there's time for.

One: but nowhere good is that close to here.

Other: somewhere bad will do.

One: really want out of here that much?

Other: need a break from the routine.

One: but don't necessarily need excitement?

Other: yeah, just some more of the mundane but in a different place.

*

One: torch song.

Other: swan song.

One: song of the south.

Other: don't go there.

One: siren song.

Other: can't come back from there.

*

Other: didn't mean to break any hearts.

One: it's nobody's fault.

Other: it's just earthquakes and plate tectonics. The lines were drawn.

One: the heart is just another epicenter. Blame the rest on geology.

Other: gravity's fault?

One: maybe. Is that how this stuff works?

Other: ask a therapist.

One: scientists will just confuse what was already figured out in simpler terms.

*

One: is this for real?

Other: well, it's not for imaginary.

One: could be for symbolic.

Other: it's all symbolic even when it's real.

One: and where's that leave the imaginary?

Other: shit out of luck.

*

Other: first love was a mistake or a miracle can't really recall.

One: don't lie.

Other: OK, it was both and it is remembered all too well.

One: and a second chance was too much too take? Don't lie.

Other: there was a third chance too.

*

One: is this love?

Other: it is a puzzle.

One: that's missing pieces.

Other: maybe. Won't know till it's all finished.

One: at least the borders are all done.

*

Other: it's hard to say.

One: it's harder not to.

Other: no sense in bottling it up.

One: might as well let it all out.

Other: well, not all. Just the important stuff.

One: oh, nothing is important.

Other: don't be a nihilist. Not now.

One: how about an absurdist?

Other: maybe just don't be.

One: that's one way to go.

Other: it's certainly gone.

One: once gone, there will be nothing else to say or at least nobody to say it to.

Other: what a relief.

*

One: every day feels longer than **the** one before it.

Other: one day, a day will be a week.

*

Other: moss grows on the south side of a tree in the southern hemisphere and north side in the northern.

One: mostly. Mostly it's about the sun.

Other: so moss grows on the sunny side?

One: yup.

Other: well, that's no help unless one is trying to go towards the light.

One: well, who isn't?

*

One: ghosts should talk more about the experience nearest to death and less about the life that was left behind.

Other: give the living all the juicy details.

One: something to consider as the end feels closest.

Other: in case somebody is thinking about bringing the end about sooner than expected.

Other: if it's peaceful, the suffering deserve to know.

One: maybe put off decisions. Be in no rush if it's miserable. Be in no rush even if it's not. Save the best for the absolute last.

Other: live through episode after episode to get to the finale. Hate watch but still loyal to the characters if not the story.

*

Other: personal purity.

One: vs the shared world.

One: sometimes it's alright to just get over it.

Other: stay as close to the heart of the ethic as possible.

One: the world will get in the way. It can't help itself, at least not right this second but things change by the minute.

*

One: everybody should be able to die for at least a few minutes.

Other: can't do that. All anybody gets is a glorified nap and then it's back to business.

*

Other: is this love?

One: it's more than that. It's survival.

*

"Talk too much for too long" (DMX)

Prologue: the after becomes the before and it is always the end of the day. And when time becomes darkest in one's own thoughts and is free to roam, those thoughts will always go towards another. Existence has already existed elsewhere and is also soon come there also. Space lays out space for crossing paths. The intersections are bright though not lit. The liminal survives in a gray tranquility. Serenity is brilliant but not so specific. Together is defined in degrees. With is a shade.

KENNING JP GARCÍA is the author of the prose works, *Furthermore and Of (What Place Meant)*, as well as the speculative poetry epics - ROBOT, *Yawning on the Sands, and Past and Again*. JP is an Afro-Absurdist diarist, antipoet, and memester. Xe is also an editor at Rigorous and Dream Pop Press.

Lightning Source UK Ltd.
Milton Keynes UK
UKHW020642231221
396134UK00010B/747